ORGANISATION FOR ADULT EDUCATION

Organisation for adult education

Graham Mee

Longman
London and New York

Longman Group Limited London

Associated companies, branches and representatives throughout the world

Published in the United States of America by Longman Inc., New York

© Longman Group Limited 1980

First published 1980

British Library Cataloguing in Publication Data

Mee, Graham
  Organisation for adult education.
  1. Adult education – Great Britain
  2. Universities and colleges – Great Britain – Administration
  374   LC5256.G7   80–40384

  ISBN 0–582–49701–9

Printed in Great Britain by
McCorquodale (Newton) Ltd., Newton-le-Willows, Lancashire.

To Susan, Richard, Steven and Hazel, for their future

Contents

Acknowledgements

We are grateful to the following for permission to reproduce copyright material:
Holt, Rinehart and Winston Inc. for extracts by G. Watson from *The Planning of Change* edited by W. Bennis *et al.*, 1970; Macmillan, London and Basingstoke and Humanities Press Inc. for our figs. 5, 6 & 7 based on *Professions and Power* by T. J. Johnson; McCutchan Publishing Corp. for our fig. 3 from *The Dynamics of Planned Educational Change* by R. E. Herriot and N. Gross *et al.*, Berkeley, © 1979; Author's agent and Random House Inc. for 2 figs. and extracts from *Beyond The Stable State*; Public and Private Learning in a Changing Society by Donald Schon, Copyright © Donald Schon 1971. Reprinted by permission of Random House Inc.

'There is perhaps no branch of our vast education system which should more attract within its particular sphere the aid and encouragement of the State than adult education.'

(Winston Churchill in a letter to the TUC in 1953)

'We believe that expenditure on adult education is one of the most purposeful and productive aspects of all education expenditure.'

(Dr Rhodes Boyson, Under-Secretary of State for Education and Science, *Hansard*, 17 January 1980)

Introduction

This is not a textbook on organisation theory. It is an attempt to look at the organisation of adult education, particularly, but not solely, in the LEA sector, using concepts and analytical frameworks taken from such theory. It has been generated by a growing conviction that organisationally much of the adult education service is ill-equipped to provide for the future demands to be made on it – indeed often it seems hardly appropriate for its current tasks. Additionally, the practitioner is frequently frustrated by his work experience; arbitrating between the conflicting demands of routine administration and development, student or teacher interests and the system of rules and regulations, home and work, can result in unsatisfactory compromises and subterfuge.

Such views have been conditioned by many years of teaching practitioners on Masters and Diploma courses in the University of Nottingham, strengthened by further contacts on summer schools and conferences. Strong reinforcement has come from a three-year research programme assessing the structure and organisation of the local education authority adult education service.[1] These teaching and research origins relate to the two central purposes of the book:

1. to provide a theoretical framework within which adult educators can better understand their work experience;
2. to identify the characteristics of organisation which are appropriate to the tasks facing adult education at present and in the future, that is to move towards a new theory and practice of adult education organisations.

There may be a measure of incompatibility between these purposes. The practitioner is likely to be impatient of theory which makes excessive use of jargon, to be rapidly discouraged by concepts which are not easily understood and seen to be relevant. Theory building can be a somewhat abstract, academically self-indulgent process, the results of which are sometimes barely comprehensible even to other academics working in the same discipline. Where a conflict between the needs of the practitioner and theory became apparent there was no difficulty in making a choice – I am on the side of the practitioner. The theory has to be accessible to those who might put it to good use. Thus it is grounded in practice – indeed current practice is not infrequently ahead of theory, pointing the way forward. The result is unlikely to satisfy organisational theorists but I am content that it should be judged by adult education practitioners.

It will already be apparent that this work owes a great debt to practitioners. Much of the content has been generated by the participation which characterises much adult teaching and I suspect that I have learned much more from students than they have from me. This would seem to be an appropriate balance in such an undertaking, for adult education is a practice, though one sorely in need of unifying theories in, for example, the sociology of organisations and adult learning. The service is operating not just in an expanding but in a changing and indefinite market, a situation implicit in the confused debate surrounding such concepts as community education, recurrent education and continuing education. Now is an appropriate time to evaluate the structures which exist and assess their relevance for the future; building adult education organisations needs to be informed by relevant theory rather than generalised philosophy.

Though the effectiveness of existing organisations can be questioned I do not jump to the conclusion that the development of a wider based service lies wholly outside of organisations; they may be inadequate but they are not irrelevant. In any case they will not wither away. There is a middle ground to be filled here between existing organisations and the views of those who would de-institutionalise the service. An alternative system has to be built which makes institutions and their resources responsive to the broadest possible range of adult education needs. What is required is a functional adult education system utilising existing resources in a co-ordinated and collective manner. Separatism has to be replaced by joint enterprise.

The reader should be aware of the personal commitments which underlie the arguments presented. I start from the belief that adults have a right to education; in a democratic society it is at best extremely shortsighted to deny that right and at worst it threatens the very continuance of the system. Therefore an education service for adults should be provided out of the public purse, or at least subsidised to that point where it is available to all adults who wish to use it; inability to pay must not prevent access. Additionally, I believe that it should be more accessible to those who have benefited least from public education provision in the past: I applaud discrimination and compensation rather than open-entry:

> The simplest answer to the 'for whom?' part of the question . . . is, 'For all who wish to take part.' This is an expression of a concept of open-entry, of a non-selective principle of recruitment. It is grounded in the general conviction that in a civilised society every adult should have access to [education] . . ., and in the specific contention that in a democratic society every citizen should have a right to use an educational service which is made possible by the deployment of public funds.
>
> The *Compensation* concept challenges this directly and claims that this allegedly non-selective open-entry system is in practice highly selective and by no means open. . . . To counter these tendencies a policy of positive discrimination is proposed. Since resources are limited they should be channelled away from those who have most and towards those who have least . . .[2].

The need for a publicly provided service has become increasingly important in the context of the traumatic changes which face society in the last two decades of the twentieth century. If men and women are to cope with these changes, if the social system is to survive, then we need a comprehensive education service for adults. Possibly we should remind ourselves of John Stuart Mill's contention that 'a state which dwarfs its men will find that with small men no great thing can really be accomplished'.[3]

Individual men and women must be given the opportunity to develop their abilities and talents in order to be able not only to cope at a personal level but also to make the maximum possible contribution to the necessarily collective responses to the challenges which face society.

At the level of actual practice I believe that what takes place under the banner of adult education should be a matter for joint determination by practitioners and actual and *potential* participants. The problem is that actual participants represent an articulate and easily consulted vested interest, whereas non-participants are by definition much less accessible and are unlikely to see the service as being relevant to their needs and aspirations. This is to see adult education as a learning system; negotiating the content of adult education is an essential educational process for the practitioner and the structures within which, and from which, he works. It is, of course, also educational for the potential user of the service. Thus the adult educator develops himself through his work and this serves to identify another important value: I am committed to the view that work should be a self-actualising experience permitting the exercise of self-determination and the fullest use of human talents. Such a belief about work is at one with my own view about the nature and purpose of adult education.

In order to make the book more readable two specific devices have been adopted. All references and notes have been kept to a necessary minimum and placed at the end of each chapter, and end-of-chapter summaries have been provided.

Where the term 'adult educator' is used it refers to an organiser with responsibility for organising a programme of educational activities for adults. It will be apparent where I am referring to others engaged in the adult service, such as administrators or teachers.

My debt to adult education practitioners had already been acknowledged. Among my university colleagues it is appropriate to identify the major influence which Professor Emeritus Harold Wiltshire has had on my approach. It would also be appropriate to acknowledge the strong influence which the work of Professor Donald A. Schon has had on the ideas presented. Finally a thank you to my wife Eileen and to my family who have once again tolerated the writer's moods with affection and good humour.

GRAHAM MEE
Department of Adult Education
University of Nottingham
January 1980

REFERENCES

1. Mee, G. and Wiltshire, H. (1978) *Structure and Performance in Adult Education*, Longman: London.
2. *Ibid*. p. 13.
3. Mill, J. S. (1859) *On Liberty*, London.

CHAPTER ONE
Crisis in adult education

It might be as well for adult education if I turned my attention to other concerns; apparently each time the desire to examine the service becomes too strong to resist a crisis develops. Thus in 1976, towards the end of the three-year research programme into LEA provision jointly conducted with Harold Wiltshire, our attention was increasingly drawn by practitioners to the ailing condition of the service. It was not initially a focus of the enquiry but increasingly it claimed our attention. The evidence was all around and could not be ignored. As a result of severe economies and sharp increases in fees charged to students, the decline in enrolments nationally in one year was 11 per cent, probably amounting to over 150,000 students. In terms of student hours the loss was probably as much as 30 per cent as organisers attempted to mitigate the effects of increases in the hourly rate of fee by reducing both the length of each class meeting and the length of courses.

It was in this context that we posed the question, is adult education in the LEA (Local Education Authority) sector a threatened service? Three years later the answer has a prophetic ring:

We have no doubt at all that adult education is indeed under threat and that in some parts of the country its very continuance is in doubt. A new principle, that adult education should be a self-supporting leisure activity for those who can afford it, is replacing the old principle that adult education should be part of the publicly funded service. This is a shift in policy in some authorities which has encountered little organised criticism or opposition and may, therefore, prove to be irreversible.[1]

In 1979, in an even harsher economic climate, the service has been suspended in Humberside and West Glamorgan. In Hampshire there will be no provision during the months of December, January and February. Clearly, the 'very continuance' of the service must be in

1

doubt for as Richard Bourne has observed, 'if they can get away with stopping at all they can get away with stopping it for good'.[2] There are of course other ways than suspension of crippling the service. By closing down most of its evening centres, by reducing or removing fee concessions for pensioners, for literacy work, etc. and by raising fees, Nottinghamshire has reduced its programme of classes by 85 per cent.

These are only some of the first, dramatic casualties resulting from the attempts of local authorities to meet Government demands for economy. But the authorities cannot blame the specific cuts on Government policy – it is their own decision to attack the adult service. The arguments usually voiced in support of such action are of the kind, 'it's either adult education or the schools'; the implication is that they are comparing like with like, but in terms of consequences this is an untenable argument. Taking say £100,000 out of the schools' budget might mean delaying a building project or cutting back sharply on new textbooks and equipment – the overall result is a marginally less effective service. Take the same amount from the adult education budget and you are likely to cripple or even destroy the service.

There is no effective trade union lobby to defend adult education. Once local authorities learn, and to some extent they already have, that they can cut the service without too much opposition, then in many areas it will cease to function except possibly as a financially self-supporting service. This new principle, which had encountered little resistance up to 1976 (or since) has continued along its inexorable path of leading to a service for those who can afford to pay. The principle need not be a matter of declared policy as it is, for example, in Surrey. All that has to happen is for a local authority steadily to reduce its budget for adult education while permitting organisers to set fee levels. Reinforced by inflation this will lead insidiously to an economic fee.

Practitioners are at fault here, whether in the universities, the WEA or the LEA sector. They have allowed the old principle of a publicly funded, or at least heavily subsidised service, to be abandoned almost without protest. It may now be too late to put into reverse the consequences of their silence. Some practitioners seem even to have embraced the self-supporting principle, possibly because they believed it was the only way to keep some kind of service going.

The acute problem in the service must not be seen as exclusive to the LEA sector; the lessons to be learned are also highly relevant to the responsible bodies. Adult education lacks the political muscle to compete for funds with other sectors of the education service. As the universities increasingly have to cope with the need to economise an early casualty is likely to be extramural work, with the arts and social sciences probably battling for survival too. If it is adult education versus engineering or science or medicine there can be only one outcome. Already some universities and the WEA (Workers' Educational Association) are feeling the effects of economies by local authorities some of whom have already reduced their grants to such bodies. Next year these grants are likely to disappear. Extramural departments and the WEA are also going to have to pay to use school premises thus adding to the pressure to increase their fees.

Mee and Wiltshire also suggested that, 'There is a real danger that adult education may be split into two segments: a heavily subsidised compensatory service for the conspicuously disadvantaged and an unsubsidised, and therefore highly priced, leisure service for the well off.'[3] What was a danger is now a reality in some areas. Faced by suspension of the service, or by severe cuts and fee increases, adult educators have usually succeeded in their fight to gain exemption for work with disadvantaged groups such as illiterates, the blind, the mentally ill, and so on. Alongside such disadvantaged provision may be found classes for which students pay as much as £1 an hour for a service which, if they lived in another county they might have for less than 30p an hour. As in other sectors of education, where you live is an important determinant of the kind of service which is available.

Practitioners are frequently put on the defensive by those who attack the service for what they see as its triviality; the flower arranging/antiques image is very persistent. It is often suggested that the service does little to meet the educational needs of the adult population. To these charges the reply must be, ask those who use the service to acquire a skill, to combat loneliness, to help compensate for their physical, mental, educational or social inadequacy; ask for example the pensioner, the widow, the single-parent family, the unemployed, the immigrant, the resident in an isolated rural community or an inner urban area, or the bored young mother. Unfortunately the views of students are rarely sought. All practitioners could cite examplers of particular students who have spoken of the value of the service to them. Only occasionally are these views expressed to a wider audience. Before her sight was restored through surgery Shiela Hocken attended adult classes in beauty care and dressmaking; her testimony is worth recording: 'It gave me a terrific feeling of completeness and of being equal to everyone else'; '. . . we all felt we had achieved something really valuable for ourselves'. Above all else, 'I suppose that the great thing about the evening classes was that they widened our confidence in our own capabilities.'[4]

Adult students do not have to be physically disabled to make such observations; feeling equal to others, achieving something really valuable to oneself and having increased confidence in one's own capabilities – these and other benefits are felt by most adult students. If the blind can see the value of the service what excuse can LEAs offer for their miserly, uncomprehending stance? Shortsightedness? They must be presented with the evidence. It is possible that the present crisis will cause students and practitioners to express their views collectively and forcibly. But other than personal testimony will be required – other kinds of evidence are essential. Here Devon County Council may be pointing the way with their recent report on the value of nursery schools at a time when many councils are cutting pre-school provision as savagely as they are adult education. 'It has found that areas in the county with few nursery school places have a larger proportion of children in need of care.' As the level of nursery provision has increased 'so demand on other services has reduced'. The conclusion of the study is that increasing preschool provision results in big savings overall both in cost and human terms.[5]

Comparable arguments have been expressed by adult educators, but the evidence has not been collected. By helping people to cope with loneliness, whether a twenty-five-year-old typist in a South Kensington bedsitter or a retired widower, what relief is provided for the health services? By developing skills and confidence in those who feel inadequate, what reduction is effected in the demand for the social services? Similarly how are the health and social services affected by the provision of a focus for community activity in an isolated rural area deprived of its bus service? By uncovering latent talents in a wide range of people, what contribution is made to the national economy? These and other relevant questions need to be researched in order to provide evidence expressed in terms of cost savings, a language likely to be understood by elected representatives in a time of financial stringency.

To those who would question whether meeting many such personal and social needs is appropriate to an education service it should be said that an educational approach, with its emphasis on the development of the individual and the group, is likely to be more effective than many of the alternatives. The latter are likely to provide a crutch rather than a possible solution through the development of latent capacities.

Adult educators must stop being defensive about the service and be more outspoken about its strengths. It should be remembered that, unlike the school system, the students are volunteers; this voluntary aspect is a testimony to the value which hundreds of thousands of adults place on the service. If the voluntary principle were introduced into the school system, I suspect that we could solve the overcrowded classrooms and teacher shortage problems immediately! With relatively little in the way of resources, adult educators are often expected to compensate for many, if not all, of the failings of schooling. If the service is to be attacked for failing to attract most of the adult population then it should be acknowledged that an important reason is that most adults have been put off education for life by their school experience. Those in the service know its limitations, appreciate and question its middle-class bias. That is not a reason for its demise but for *change*. More resources are needed, not less. Adult educators have already shown in the literacy programme what they can achieve with relatively limited extra resources and support. It is precisely in the same area that the irresponsibility of some local authorities has been most sharply demonstrated through their decision to suspend literacy work or to charge fees to those benefiting from such programmes. It is unlikely that the reaction of some part-time adult literacy co-ordinators, who have agreed to work for no pay rather than abandon their students, will shame the authorities concerned into a rethink.

It is a paradox in a democratic society that where individuals, in large numbers, vote directly for a particular kind of public expenditure it can be cut without reference to them. They 'vote' by enrolling, and usually reinforce this by being prepared to contribute more than their rates and taxes by paying a fee. Effectively there has been an annual referendum on the public provision of adult education and over 1·5 million 'voters' have said yes.

The present situation must raise the question, are LEAs to be entrusted with the responsibility imposed by Section 41 of the 1944 Education Act?

It shall be the duty of every local education authority to secure the provision for their area of adequate facilities for further education, that is to say: (a) full-time and part-time education for persons over compulsory school age; and (b) leisure time occupation in such organised cultural training and recreative activities as are suited to their requirements, for any persons over compulsory school age who are able and willing to profit by the facilities provided for that purpose.

Unless a case is brought to test whether some LEAs are defaulting on their statutory duties the service is likely to continue to decline. However, even if a test case were successful, it is questionable whether it would be very helpful; 'adequate' provision might still permit of a very limited service. It is not minimum compliance which is needed but a commitment to the *spirit* of the Act.

More usefully Parliament could tighten the legislation. It could recognise how illogical it is to cut the adult service at a time when the demand is increasing and will continue to do so at an accelerating rate in the remainder of this century and beyond. Declining provision has to be seen against a background in which growth is the norm. The demand for adult education has been rising in the last three decades as a direct and inevitable result of the growth and extension of initial education. Moreover we are persistently told, and the evidence is at hand, that we must prepare ourselves for the inescapable consequences of new technology: even greater unemployment, reduction in the working week, earlier retirement and the need for retraining. In this context a strong adult education service is essential. Now is precisely the time for it to be developed and expanded. Instead, it is being dramatically contracted and is becoming a service for the well-off and the conspicuously disadvantaged; there will be nothing for that great middle mass of the population who will be markedly affected by technological change. At its crudest central government initiative in adult education is needed to help 'buy' social peace in an era of increasing disruption in the lives of men and women.

If the present service, whatever its shortcomings, is allowed to die, there will be a dissipation of the very talent which could be the springboard for take-off into this new and demanding phase of development of an education service for all adults, whatever their needs. Adult educators understand adults, their needs and learning difficulties, and in this rapidly changing world we need them to lead, to advise and to counsel. The new comprehensive service which they have to create will be very different from the service of today, but given the appropriate organisational framework within which to function the necessary changes can be made, providing that is, resources are made available. This book is largely concerned with that framework, with identifying the necessary organisational characteristics of a flexible, adaptive education service for adults. Though it is written at a time of crisis, it expresses the firm conviction that there will be a dramatic extension of the adult service in the 1980s. The alternatives, of a service which continues to contract or one which stands still, are untenable and too threatening in terms of their consequences.

REFERENCES

1. Mee, G. and Wiltshire, H. (1978) *Structure and Performance in Adult Education*. Longman: London, p. 112.
2. Bourne, R. 'Too old to learn', *The Guardian*, 4.9.1979.

3. Mee and Wiltshire, *op. cit.*, p. 112.
4. Hocken, S. (1978) *Emma and I*. Sphere: London, Ch. 8.
5. Stevens, A. 'Nurseries cut cost of care', *The Observer*, 4.11.1979.

CHAPTER TWO

Understanding organisations

WHY STUDY ORGANISATIONS?

We live in an organisation society. Our lives are largely played out in such organisational roles as employee, student and patient. In the modern welfare state it is highly likely that we will come into this world in a hospital and take leave of it in some organisation specialising in the care of the elderly. Organisations provide the goods and services we consume and use. The food that we eat is processed, packaged, canned, distributed and sold by organisations. Local authorities remove our refuse, clean the streets, provide schools and build houses; other public authorities provide our systems of communication. In order to buy what we consume we work in organisations and eventually retire from them.

It is difficult to find any facet of life which is not organised for us. Even our leisure time, linked with increases in disposable income, has generated a new industry made up of such organisations as radio and television companies, travel agencies, holiday camps, ferry and air charter companies and leisure centres.

For its part, education as at present conceived is a highly organised service requiring extensive investment in plant and equipment and a very large workforce. The statutory age for entering school is five, though many children experience organisational life before this in play schools or nursery schools. Until the age of sixteen the law requires a child's continuing attendance at school beyond which he can remain in the student role from two years upwards, in school, college or university.

Adult education, though commanding a small proportion of total expenditure on education, is no less an organised service. In Britain most is provided by local authorities using school and college premises; much of the rest by university extramural departments, polytechnics and the Workers' Educational Association. This raises an important issue. In most of our contacts with organisations we have little choice but to buy their products or use their services – we may choose between this product and that, between self-service and personal service but in the end, for example, we do have to eat and we do take a holiday. But we do not have to use an adult education service; adults are, usually, volunteer students whose perception of the service will be affected by the type of organisation they must enter or relate to. Typically this will be a school, a structure from which most 'escaped' many years before and which they are unlikely to re-enter voluntarily; if a college or university, these will be seen by most as organisations to which others go, places to which bright pupils go after school life. Suggestions by the providers that adult education is different, that it is not like 'going back to school,' are likely to be ineffectual in combating an attitude built-in by a decade's experience of education. As Ackoff suggests, 'most schools appear to put a lid on children's minds. Curiosity and creativity are suppressed. Learning is equated to memorisation, thus converting it into work and differentiating it from play. Only a relatively few are ever able to reunite work, play and learning in later life.'[1] Similarly Flude and Parrott have observed that, 'Students would like to leap into jobs from the school gate. Their disablement is from education itself. They are disabled from any return to learning because the idea that learning is a valuable skill has been discredited by its context.'[2]

But adult education is a publicly subsidised service avowedly open to all, though in effect only a relatively small proportion of the adult population make use of it. The reluctance of the majority to use the service may be due to many causes but it is a basic assumption of this book *that important among these is its organisation*. Existing organisations and the service they provide may simply be discouraging, they lack relevance and appeal. New or modified structures are needed which help to make adult education provision accessible and relevant. Although the focus is organisations I am not advocating only that we need to change structures – it is also necessary to change what we do and how and where we do it. In this I find myself broadly in agreement with the view that,

. . . adult educators need to find more adequate reasons that 'a lack of confidence to come forward' or a generated disapproval of school education to explain the lack of take-up of the educational opportunities in adult education among working class adults. The individualism of adult education itself and a curriculum which reflects middle class life styles may be a sufficient deterrent in themselves.[3]

Nevertheless it is maintained that unless the way adult education is organised is appropriate it is unlikely that the other changes which are necessary are ever going to be made.

We need, therefore, to study organisations not simply to understand them but to improve them or, more positively, to change them: improvement implies some change in relation to existing tasks whereas in adult education new publics and new tasks represent a challenge which existing structures are unlikely to be able to meet. Change of a fundamental nature is needed.

WHAT ARE THE CHARACTERISTICS OF AN ORGANISATION?

So far we have assumed a general understanding of the term organisation, but what are the characteristics which schools, hospitals, industrial firms, local authority departments and so on, have in common which enable us to use the concept organisation to describe all of them? Basically they are all purposive social systems which exist to achieve more or less specific goals. The concept of organisational goal is usually taken as the defining characteristic. Thus for Etzioni, 'organisations are social units deliberately constructed and reconstructed to seek specific goals.'[4] Blau and Scott make the same point; an organisation is, 'a social unit that has been established for the explicit purpose of achieving certain goals.'[5] Etzioni further suggests that goals serve several functions:

They provide orientation by depicting a future state of affairs which the organisation strives to realise. Thus they set down guidelines for organisational activity. Goals also constitute a source of legitimacy which justifies the activities of an organisation and, indeed, its very existence. Moreover goals serve as standards by which members of an organisation and outsiders can assess the success of the organisation. . . . Goals also serve in a similar fashion as measuring rods for the student of organisations who trys to determine how well the organisation is doing.[6]

In attempting to achieve their goals organisations will have a rationally defined structure. There will be a hierarchy of authority and a division of labour within which each member will have a more or less prescribed function. Work tasks will be performed within a written framework of rules and regulations. By structuring the organisation around such principles those persons filling positions at the apex of the hierarchy attempt to co-ordinate and control the work of the other members. Schein summarises this orthodox or bureaucratic view of organisations as follows: 'An organisation is the rational co-ordination of the activities of a number of people for the achievement of some common explicit purpose or goal, through division of labour and function, and through a hierarchy of authority and responsibility.'[7] Although most readers would recognise these characteristics of organisations such a definition is inadequate in many ways. The defining concept goal is value laden – whose goals are we talking about? Implicitly management's, that is those at the top of the organisation's hierarchy. To suggest that those occupying subordinate positions will automatically accept these as the only goals to be served, or even as the most important goals, defies our experience of organisations. Consensus in this area cannot be assumed, indeed it is more realistic and helpful to assume conflict. Again the idea of a single purpose organisation is something which challenges reality and it is more meaningful to conceive of a system with multiple purposes, open to and interacting with other systems in its environment.

In this way the direction in which an organisation moves can be seen as resulting from a conflict of forces both inside and outside of itself:

All formal organisations are moulded by forces tangential to their rationally ordered structures and stated goals. Every formal organisation – trade union, political party, army, corporation, etc. – attempts to mobilise human and technical resources as means for the achievement of its ends. However, the individuals within the system tend to resist being treated as means. They interact as wholes, bringing to bear their own special problems and purposes; moreover the organisation is embedded in an institutional matrix and is therefore subject to pressure upon it from its environment, to which some general adjustment must be made. As a result, the organisation may be significantly viewed as an adaptive social structure, facing problems which arise simply because it exists as an organisation in an institutional environment, independently of the special (economic, military, political) goals which called it into being.[8]

This combination of pressures modifies and changes organisational goals. For their part organisational members have their own values and priorities which they will attempt to express in their work but the freedom to do so will be constrained not only by the organisation and its other members but by its relations with the public which it serves and by other organisations with which it relates. These relationships will be expressed in a complex pattern of overlapping social networks.

Where the balance will be struck between organisational requirements, individual needs, and the interests of other organisations and the public will depend on such factors as the degree of centralisation, the degree of autonomy granted to the individual member and the bargaining power of other organisations and the public. Some structures are highly decentralised with sub-units operating in *'frontline'* situations in which members can take personal initiatives which are not easily supervised from the centre and which are not visible to others not directly involved. Social work organisation, for example, has this characteristic. Attempts by senior officers to restrict the autonomy of the individual social worker through professional training, case conferences and insistence on regular written reports can only modify but not change the frontline nature of the work.

Some organisations are more vulnerable to external influences than others. To use a biological analogy, it is useful here to see any organisation as an open system surrounded by a 'semi-permeable membrane' or boundary. Its degree of permeability or openness will depend on the type of organisation and the actions of those members who control access, that is those who perform what can be described as boundary roles with power to open or close the 'gate'. A prison is an example of a type of organisation which is largely shut off from its environment, whose boundary is physically visible with its members isolated behind gates and walls; access (and egress) is subject to strict control. In complete contrast to such custodial structures are voluntary organisations with few, if any, restrictions on entry, such as the Townswomen's Guild, the YMCA, the YHA, or Friends of the Earth. Here boundaries are best understood as perceptions in people's minds: whether I join or not depends on whether I see it as my kind of organisation expressing values with which I agree and conducting activities which interest me. Such organisations are likely to be highly vulnerable to outside pressures.

So far the concept social network has been used without any attempt at definition:

A network is a set of elements related to one another through multiple interconnections. The metaphor of the net suggests a special kind of interconnectedness, one dependent on nodes in which several connecting strands meet. There is the suggestion both of each element being connected to every other, and of elements connecting through one another rather than to each other through a centre.

Where social, organisational or interpersonal networks are in question, there is the concept of channels of relationship among elements, which make it easier or more likely for transactions of a certain kind to occur among elements than if those channels were not present. There is, then, the notion of flows or processes which occur preferentially within the network. In the first instance, networks can be defined through the nature of channels connecting them (formal lines of authority, information or decision; interpersonal bonds) and the nature of the transactions that can occur through these channels (in this sense, there may be 'referral', 'early warning', 'distribution', or 'money-lending' networks).[9]

A map of the networks within which an organisation is set and with which it interacts is likely to be extremely complex. Nevertheless such a map is essential to an understanding of the way an organisation functions, to the how and the why of decision-making and to any attempt to change the organisation. The networks in which a full-time education organiser in the LEA sector is likely to be functioning will include not only other organisers, administrative officers, teachers and students but also local councillors, school staff, the youth service, the caring services, voluntary organisations and agencies, local officers of government departments, industry and trade unions, local societies, the media, the WEA and the local university, etc.

ORGANISATIONAL CONCEPTS AND ADULT EDUCATION

Typically existing adult education structures demonstrate the essential characteristics of the traditional organisation model such as hierarchical decision-making, prescribed functions and a system of rules and regulations. It is, therefore, difficult to argue with Lovett's observation that,

Adult education, like any other 'community' service, is, in a great majority of instances, typified by a hierarchical structure and bureaucratic organisation. Although it often stresses its informality, this is mainly a matter of teaching technique – and not always then – and the relationship between teacher and taught. Structurally it implies a less formal teaching arrangement. However, this is almost always confined to the classroom.
In practice adult education has a very formal structure typical of most organisations. The nature of the service (education) is decided, with few exceptions, by those in control. . . .
The criterion for judging success in such an institutional setting is normally that which satisfies the bureaucratic concern for order and statistics, i.e. formal classes and a register of those attending. All the bureaucratic paraphernalia of registers and forms are, therefore, much in evidence.[10]

The service, as presently conceived, is provided in schools, colleges and extra-mural departments of universities, or in some out-station of such institutions, all of which are hierarchically structured with prescribed work roles related either to administrative function or to subject specialism. Even where an adult centre is detached from a host institution it operates, like any other adult education organisation, within a complex, hierarchically administered local authority or university. The WEA probably has the least complex organisation, though there are both national and district structures which practitioners are likely to experience as a constraining framework.

The criteria used to evaluate success in adult education are almost wholly administrative; usually, for example, budget is dependent on enrolment. Educational criteria are rarely applied. The problem is one of control and accountability and the consequent need of those who provide resources to measure the efficiency of organisations. Unfortunately some achievements are more easily measured than others; the consequences of this are succinctly expressed by Etzioni:

> ... measuring can distort the organisational efforts [where] some aspects of its output are more measurable than the others. Frequent measuring tends to encourage over-production of highly measurable items and neglect of the less measurable ones. . . .
>
> The distortion consequences of over-measuring are larger when it is impossible to quantify the more central, substantive output of an organisation, and when at the same time some exterior aspects of the product, which are superficially related to its substance, are readily measurable.[11]

To illustrate his argument he takes the case of schools which measure success on the basis of examination passes to the neglect of the 'character development' of their students.

Such arguments are highly relevant to adult education. In general those who employ adult educators judge their success on the readily measurable number of students catered for, or the number of classes provided. Such an evaluative process is often reflected in the actual salaries paid to practitioners, particularly heads of centre in the LEA sector employed on a part-time basis. They are usually paid by results, that is by the number of students enrolled and/or the total of classes organised. More students, at least until the financial cutbacks of the 1970s, meant more income. It is only to be expected that in this situation there will be a strong motivation to provide popular classes which enrol well. It does not pay to experiment in unusual or minority interest areas. This tendency is reinforced where the employer insists on a minimum enrolment of as many as fifteen students before a class may begin. In the past further reinforcement has come from the generally accepted formula that a centre achieving an enrolment of over 1000 students justified a full-time appointment. (I would not wish to suggest that centre-heads' sole or even prime motivation is to maximise their incomes and budgets, only that there are significant pressures which do not encourage an innovatory attitude.)

Though a few employing authorities have shown greater imagination in evaluating the service the message for practitioners is usually quite explicit; if you cannot measure it it does not count; if you lose students/classes your budget will be cut. In this context what chance is there of applying such qualitative criteria as a 'balanced' programme, the development of student potential or the effectiveness of learning? Goal distortion of the kind identified by Etzioni would appear to be inherent in existing adult education structures. Extramural departments and the WEA are little different here. Their annual reports are replete with lists of classes and the numbers enrolled in each one; quorum numbers are applied before classes can begin and if attendance falls below the permissible minimum closure is likely. Adult educators, in whatever kind of organisation, have to play the 'numbers game'.

Burton R. Clark has identified the dangers consequent on functioning within such an 'enrolment economy'.[12] He argues that because enrolment becomes *the* criterion the practitioner becomes very sensitive both to the demands of the established clientèle and to outside pressure groups, to the point where 'student choice determines the evolution of the curriculum'; he becomes 'situation-directed not goal-directed'. Such observations are related to a view of the service as a professionally dominated system with goals determined by adult educators. There is, of course, a strongly held counterview that control over curriculum should rest with students anyway; that student power here is consistent with basic adult education principles. Thus some might respond to Clark's conclusion by saying that it is not for the adult educator to play God but to respond to students' expressed needs. This counter-argument raises further difficulties. What of unexpressed needs? In a publicly subsidised service, what of the non-user?

There is an apparent conflict between Clark's view of student control over curriculum and Lovett's earlier quoted observation that the nature of the service is decided by those in control. Clark's point is that given the voluntary nature of student involvement the adult educator has to be sensitive to their needs – he has to attract them in large enough numbers through the provision of popular courses. Lovett would acknowledge this situation but would counter by suggesting that practitioners' control in the sense that, with few exceptions, they are only prepared to offer a standard product, that is a class: '. . . although adult education offers a range of subjects, they are almost all encompassed within a uniform, standardized system that presents no major problems for the organisation and the values it represents.'[13]

For their part most students are unlikely to be aware of the power to influence which is potentially theirs. They are, however, likely to be very conscious of 'the bureaucratic concern for order'. Enrolment, for example, can be a time-consuming and somewhat harrowing

15

experience of queueing, form filling, fee paying or gaining access to a concessionary category, and having one's name and number entered on a register. Attendance will then be necessary at a certain time and place. Particularly in the early weeks the teacher is likely to call the register until he knows the students and thereafter continue to fill it in, in order that central administration can eventually satisfy itself that attendance requirements have been complied with. Tutors and organisers have to go through these bureaucratic exercises not only with enrolment and registers but also with claims for teaching fees and travelling expenses.

Adult educators complain frequently of the constraints in such a system. Some, possibly few, may however be content to meet the administrative demands of the role, to be judged on the basis of statistics and returns. It is undoubtedly less demanding to meet the expectations of one's employer in these respects than to get involved in such leadership aspects of the role as curriculum development, community outreach and teacher supervision and support. Those who emphasise these leadership tasks would acknowledge that the system can be and has to be manipulated: the rules and regulations can be bent, though the opportunity to do so will tend to vary according to the type of institution. For many the opportunity is afforded by their frontline situation. Their relative privacy allows them to take initiatives and bend the rules often without central administrators being aware. Contact between officers and frontline practitioners is typically infrequent and the former's attempts to control the situation through registers and returns are likely to be ineffectual. Many adult educators respond to the more immediate, and for them more relevant, pressures of students and teachers. The stance taken is that of the professional educator – what is in the interests of students? If rules and regulations stand in the way they are to be manipulated; if registers and returns are a potential constraint they can be presented in a way which will ensure that central administrators are not aware of what has occurred.

Many subterfuges are employed. If a certain group activity would not be approved then find a 'class' label to describe it which officers would accept without question; if there are concessionary groups who pay a reduced fee or no fee then place students in such a category if they are unable to attend otherwise; if by educational criteria it is appropriate to run a class with x students (possibly a craft group requiring certain facilities for each member) but the rules demand say $x + 3$ enrolments then a 'ghost' list of non-fee-paying students may be used to make up the number.

The nature of this clash between professional and administrative criteria is well understood: 'the ultimate justification for a professional act is that it is, to the best of the professional's knowledge, the right act. . . . The ultimate justification of an administrative act, however, is that it is in line with the organisation's rules and regulations, and that it has been approved . . . by a superior rank.'[14] The conflict may be compounded in the LEA sector because those who make the rules are unlikely to have had experience of working in adult education. Senior education officers are typically drawn from a background of administration and teaching in schools and therefore are not likely to be seen by adult educators as appropriate persons to be making judgements about the adult sector of the service.

There will be cause to return to this theme of the freedom of the practitioner to mitigate the effects of organisation both in the informal sense referred to and as formalised authority to exercise discretion.

In manipulating rules and regulations the adult educator is operating as a 'boundary definer'. He is 'dealing with the flow and counterflow of forces between an institution and its environment', in such a way, 'as to make the boundary either more or less permeable'.[15] In this role he applies his own hierarchy of values and priorities, in so far as organisational policies and resources permit him to do so. He 'is capable not only of ignoring, accepting, modifying, mobilizing, or otherwise responding to forces that exist, but is also likely to generate or create forces that might not have existed without him'. Many practitioners have considerable freedom to determine the appropriateness for the service of particular needs or demands, to decide that an idea or activity is relevant to their function. Some are highly creative in relation to their environments, others are very passive. This difference was effectively expressed in practitioners' comments recorded by Mee and Wiltshire. One respondent, when asked if his programme provided for any kind of disadvantaged group or individual replied, 'I have never had any requests'; such passivity contrasts sharply with such observations as 'I see myself as a catalyst for developing the ideas of others', and 'I pride myself and get my kicks out of being creative'.[16]

The freedom of the adult educator to define the boundary of his institution must not be overstated. It has already been established that he operates within an 'enrolment economy', mostly he has to provide what students are prepared to pay for, although fee concessions have afforded a measure of freedom here. Whether fee payers or not, however, his students are volunteers and therefore in a strong position to influence programmes. This vulnerability to student pressure is likely to be reinforced by the imprecision which characterises attempts to define goals in adult education. Clark has suggested that the service is characterised by an 'uncommon . . . degree of goal ambiguity' which renders practitioners highly susceptible to external influences.[17] It should be noted, however, that once again Clark has a view of a professionally dominated service; he also unquestioningly adopts the goal model of organisations.

There would seem to be many possibilities for conflicting views of organisational boundary in adult education. Musgrave indicates the nature of the problem:

Possibly because the term 'boundary' has been applied in an unthinking and reified manner little attention has been given to the problematic nature of organisational boundaries. In particular it has been forgotten that boundaries do not exist 'out there' in society, but are perceptions in the minds of those filling positions in and interacting with those in the organisations concerned. Once this is realised it is clear that those concerned may hold differing perceptions of where any organisation's boundaries lie. . . . Because service organisations are by definition dealing with personal problems conflict over defining organisational boundaries would seem probable.[18]

Such conflicts over perceptions of boundaries are inevitable in adult education given the problematic nature of such concepts and issues as community education, the status of practitioners, the sharing or borrowing relationship with other institutions, the voluntary nature of student participation and the role of students in decision-making. In the latter area practitioners may have a different perception of the appropriate degree of student involvement in decision-making from the students themselves or from their employing authority. In a multipurpose institution a headmaster/principal may have a different perception of adult education from that held by the person immediately responsible for the adult programme; such an institution may be seen in terms of the 'college as community' whereas the adult educator may feel it more appropriate to operate 'out there' in the community. School or college staff attitudes expressed in references to 'my room', 'my equipment' are probably best understood in terms of boundaries of influence. In trying to develop a community role a practitioner may find himself in conflict with the perception of organisational boundary held by another institution: is it social work or adult education?

It has already been suggested that adult educators are likely to operate within a range of complex social networks. These may be formal, related, for example, to command or information; or informal, linking with persons, groups and other organisations. Informal networks are used 'to circumvent, supplement or replace the operations of formal organisational systems' and 'have long served to enable people to get things done when the formal networks failed'.[19] Increasingly many adult educators have developed the skills appropriate to building informal networks and often find themselves in nodal positions in *ad hoc* networks which have grown up 'to compensate for mismatches between the institutional map and problems perceived as important'.[20]

The networks within which practitioners operate are likely to vary according to the type of providing institution. Where such differences exist they not only reflect the conceptual view of adult education held by the institutions concerned but also provide reinforcement for such a view. In this context Musgrave has observed,

... that those who advocate community schools or deschooling or any other similar structural change in the school system must, if they wish to be successful, base their strategy upon the characteristics of the organisation that they want to change as well as those of the structure that they wish to create and upon the social networks in which the school is set and with which it interacts.[21]

Therefore any attempt to change fundamentally the kind of service which a particular type of institution offers will need to be based on an analysis of existing social networks and the identification of those likely to be most appropriate to the new role.

Such an analysis may lead, for example, to an awareness of the need for structural changes or adjustments in the method of providing the service. The range of possible initiatives is very wide. In order to widen or change social networks it might be thought appropriate to detach a worker from the centre and place him 'out there' in the community, or it may be decided to locate a much larger proportion of programme activities away from the centre in village halls, homes for the elderly, community centres, etc. The need to develop new social networks, to cope with what for many has been a new function, is well illustrated by the literacy programme; contacts with personnel officers in industry, social welfare agencies, voluntary tutors, remedial teachers, radio and the press, seem to be essential to such work.

SUMMARY AND CONCLUSION

Organisations, of whatever kind, tend to have certain characteristics in common. Essentially they are purposive social systems, existing to achieve certain goal(s). They will have a rationally defined structure based on a hierarchy of authority and specialisation of tasks. These prescribed tasks will be carried out within a framework of rules and regulations.

This goal model has serious limitations and is value-laden. It is more meaningful to conceive of an organisation as an open system interacting with other systems in its environment. It is an adaptive social structure with permeable boundaries in which organisational direction is determined by a range of internal and external pressures.

In the special case of adult education organisations the goal model seems particularly inappropriate; such concepts as permeability, boundary, social networks and frontline are more relevant to an understanding of such structures and for informing attempts at organisational change. Therefore in looking for an alternative organisation it will be important to see adult education institutions as open systems, subject to many pressures in their decision-making, rather than as goal-seeking structures. Indeed there must be serious doubts about the relevance of the goal model at all. The alternative, based on the commitment to both user and non-user involvement in goal determination and on the view that many of the educational needs of adults have yet to be uncovered, is to advocate and design not a goal model but a *learning system*. The acknowledged goal of the system is to learn, by developing the necessary social networks. Such a learning system could not be a hierarchically organised, highly centralised, goal seeking system of the orthodox kind, but a dispersed system with goals determined as the product of the learning process. Adult education has to learn to become an education service for all adults, whatever their needs and aspirations.

REFERENCES

1. Ackoff, Russell L. (1974) *Redesigning the Future: a systems approach to societal problems*, Wiley: New York, p. 73.
2. Flude, R. and Parrott, A. (1979) *Education and the Challenge of Change*, Milton Keynes, p. 44.
3. Keddie, Nell (1980) Adult education: an ideology of individualism, in Thompson, Jane L. (ed.) *Adult Education for a Change*, Hutchinson: London.
4. Etzioni, A. (1964) *Modern Organizations*, Prentice-Hall: New Jersey, p. 3.
5. Blau, P. M. and Scott, W. R. (1963) *Formal Organisations*, Routledge and Kegan Paul: London, p. 1.
6. Etzioni, p. 5.
7. Schein, Edgar H. (1965) *Organisational Psychology*, Prentice-Hall: New Jersey, p. 8.
8. Selznick, P. (1966) *TVA and the Grass Roots*, Harper and Row: New York, p. 251.

9. Schon, Donald A. (1971) *Beyond the Stable State*, M. Temple-Smith: London; Penguin: Harmondsworth, pp. 177–8.
10. Lovett, Tom (1975) *Adult Education, Community Development and the Working Class*, Ward Lock: London, p. 127.
11. Etzioni, pp. 9–10.
12. Clark, Burton R. (1958) *The Marginality of Adult Education*, Chicago Center for the Study of Liberal Education for Adults: Boston.
13. Lovett, pp. 128–9.
14. Etzioni, p. 77.
15. Deppe, Donald A. (October 1969) 'The adult educator: marginal man and boundary definer', *Adult Leadership*, **18**, (No. 4), 119–30.
16. Mee, G. and Wiltshire, H. (1978) *Structure and Performance in Adult Education*, Longman: London.
17. Clark, *op. cit.*
18. Musgrave, P. W. (October 1973) 'The relationship between school and community: a reconsideration', *Community Development Journal* **8**, (No. 3).
19. Schon, p. 178.
20. *Ibid.*, pp. 178–9.
21. Musgrave, p. 178.

CHAPTER THREE
Design principles for an education service for adults

The choice of words in the chapter title is deliberate. I do not intend to engage in debate about what is meant by adult education or by fashionable alternatives, such as continuing education, recurrent education or community education. Much of what is implicit in these labels is here taken to be adult education, that is an *education service for all adults*, whatever demands they would wish to make on a publicly provided or subsidised service. What is needed is a service for *adult persons, not for children or adolescents*. Its environment must be adult, both physically and psychologically; its methodology and content must be appropriate to adults.

There are two possible approaches to the designing of such a service:

1. *We could create a grand design* – starting from scratch we could produce an organisational blueprint, an ideal system.

2. Alternatively we could *start from where we are* – take existing organisational structures and change them in appropriate ways.

It is intended to explore both possibilities. A case for evolving a grand design, an ideal system, can be made out. At the same time it has to be accepted that much of the service will continue to be provided from existing organisations, that is by LEAs, universities, polytechnics and the WEA. Such a view finds support in a recent ACACE (Advisory Council for Adult and Continuing Education) document which maintains that 'It should be assumed that the provision would come largely from existing organisations.'[1] Although it is conventional to demigrate much of the adult education work of such structures they are not going to wither away, there is too much investment in capital and human resources. Those who seek to revolutionise the service attack its programme and institutional base, offering alternatives built round such concepts as community or continuing education. Though interesting, titles for conferences, in general discussion of such concepts often serves only to detract from the essentials of the debate: *how do we build an education service appropriate for adults – open, accessible and relevant to all adults?*

Those who attack what they regard as traditional adult education tend to ignore its many achievements. A strong, if traditional, class programme often seems to provide a firm foundation from which adult educators have developed activity in new areas. Again it has drawn new clientèle from among the ranks of the educationally, economically, socially, physically or mentally disadvantaged. Additionally, though there is undoubtedly a core curriculum in adult education,[2] the service has demonstrated an ability to respond to changing demands, though admittedly these tend to come from articulate members of the community.

It is my belief that the architects of new grand designs have found themselves the wrong labels. To most adults continuing or recurrent education can only be perceived through a set of attitudes conditioned by a decade of schooling; the last thing most adults would volunteer for is a continuation or a recurrence of what they have already experienced as education. There is a massive task here of enabling adults to unlearn deep-seated attitudes. The difficulty is compounded when much adult education, whatever the label, is seen to take place in schools or colleges or universities. Ideally an adult service would have the resources to grow on its own terms, unencumbered by a dependent little-brother relationship with a school or college – there is often little that is adult or worldly in such environments.

The two approaches adopted here have been conceptualised by Ackoff as *preactivism* and *interactivism*:

Preactivists seek change *within* the system, but not change *of* the system or its environment. They are reformers not revolutionaries.

On the other hand,

Interactivists are not willing to settle for the current state of affairs or the way they are going. . . . They want to design a desirable future and invent ways of bringing it about. . . .

Preactivists, according to interactivists spend too much time trying to forecast the future. The future, they argue, depends more on what we do between now and then than it does on what has happened up until now. . . . The interactive planner initiates ends planning by designing an *idealised future* for the systems being planned for. This is a design of the future which begins 'from scratch.' . . .

Most system planning is retrospective, preoccupied with identifying and removing deficiencies in the past performance of system components. Retrospective planning moves *from* what one does not want rather than toward what one wants.[3]

Organisation for adult education

It is intended here to use a preactive and an interactive approach in a mutually supportive way; there is need for both reform and revolution. By 'starting from scratch' the characteristics of an ideal system can be identified which may then be used in a preactive way to suggest directions for change within the existing system. This would appear to be consistent with Ackoff's view of interactivists as people who 'pursue ideals that they know can never be attained but that can be continuously approached'.[4]

BUILDING AN ADULT ORGANISATION: AN IDEAL SYSTEM

What would be the characteristics of an *adult* organisation? That is a structure which reflects the needs and aspirations of adults as learners and which itself is a learning system. Like persons, organisations also need to learn and develop in relevant directions. Starting from scratch in this way enables the designer to utilise theory generated in such disciplines as psychology, organisation theory and management theory.

Principles of job design

Our starting point is personality theory: what are the characteristics of the adult person and are they consonant with the demands of organisational life? The views of man held by management theorists have developed in this century from the concept of man as a rational economic being, through man as a social being to what Schein identifies as complex man.[5] The root of the latter view is to be found in the work of Maslow[6] who identified a hierarchy of needs which provide the motivating force for human behaviour. These needs can be expressed as follows:

- basic physiological needs for food, sex, shelter, etc.
- safety needs for protection from danger and threat of deprivation
- social and affiliative needs: the need for love and a sense of belonging
- ego or status needs: the need for self-esteem and the esteem of others
- self-actualisation needs for creativity and the opportunity for fulfilling one's potential.

Maslow's needs hierarchy, developed by such authors as Argyris,[7] McGregor,[8] and Hertzberg,[9] has provided the essential base for the personality versus organisation hypothesis – the contention that there is a fundamental conflict between organisational and human needs. It is maintained that the personality needs of the mature individual for independence, challenge and variety are largely, or even wholly, frustrated by the organisation's need for compliance within a hierarchically structured decision-making system based on division of labour and specialisation. The degree to which such frustration is experienced by any particular individual within the organisation will depend on such factors as the nature of his work and his position in the hierarchy. Nevertheless although the idea of a necessary and fundamental conflict, and the consequent recommendations of appropriate managerial and organisational strategies, have been subject to these and other criticisms[10] there is broad agreement that the hypothesis constitutes a major step in our understanding of the relationship between man and organisation. Indeed it has led not only to many prescriptions for job redesign but also to their actual application.

The broad consensus in this area is reflected in Emery and Thorsrud's conclusion that, 'Cumulative investigations in Europe, North America, Australia and Scandinavia have enabled social scientists to identify a number of important determinants of job satisfaction' as follows:

1. Adequate elbow room. The sense that they are their own bosses and that except in exceptional circumstances they do not have some boss breathing down their necks. Not so much elbow room that they just don't know what to do next.
2. Chances of learning on the job and going on learning. We accept that such learning is possible only when men are able to set goals that are reasonable challenges for them and get a feedback of results in time for them to correct their behaviour.
3. An optimal level of variety, i.e. they can vary the work so as to avoid boredom and fatigue and so as to gain the best advantages from settling into a satisfactory rhythm of work.
4. Conditions where they can and do get help and respect from their workmates . . .
5. A sense of one's work meaningfully contributing to social welfare . . .
6. A desirable future. Quite simply not a dead end job; hopefully one that will continue to allow personal growth.[11]

They conclude that these psychological requirements *cannot* be met by 'simply fiddling with individual job specifications, e.g. job enlargement, job rotation, rest pauses, humane supervision contacts'; the answer lies in 'locating responsibility, for control over effort and quality of personal work and for interpersonal co-ordination, with the people who are actually doing the job'.

Organisation for adult education

Although such findings have been largely generated by research in industrial settings both their relevance for the design of jobs in educational organisations and their close links with learning theory will not be lost on the reader. Both organiser and student are adult learners and the above determinants of work satisfaction are relevant to both. Thus adult education organisations need to structure work roles and learning methodologies consonant with these needs for *autonomy, challenge and a chance to go on learning, variety, mutual support and respect, meaningfulness and a desirable future.*

Learning systems

Learning adults need to work in a learning system. Schon sees our existing organisational systems as 'memorials to old problems', and maintains that 'our need is to develop institutional structures, ways of knowing, and an ethic for the process of change itself'.[12] 'We must . . . become adept at learning. We must become able not only to transform our institutions, in response to changing situations and requirements; we must invent and develop institutions which are "learning systems", that is to say, systems capable of bringing about their own continuing transformation.' Few adult educators would argue (within their own field) that, 'no established institution in our society now perceives itself as adequate to the challenges that face it'. But what are the characteristics of an organisational system for the education of adults?

Schon tells us that 'the movement towards learning systems is of necessity a groping and inductive process for which there is no adequate theoretical base'.[13] He sees the traditional organisational model as being centre–periphery model is a 'constellation' structure in which allocation from a centralised structure: innovation occurs as a result of decisions made at the centre (Fig. 1). An elaboration of the 'centre–periphery' model is a 'constellation' structure in which secondary centres are differentiated from the primary centre but the latter maintains control (Fig. 2).[14]

Existing adult education organisations are centre–periphery structures. Resources are centrally controlled and allocated and innovation is a matter for decision-making within centres, colleges or departments. This is not to suggest that such decisions are not influenced by external pressures – the essential factor is that whatever those pressures decision-making is a process which occurs within the organisation with its ability to control resource allocation.

Developing his proliferation of centres model Schon maintains that: 'The model of the proliferation of centres makes of the primary centre a

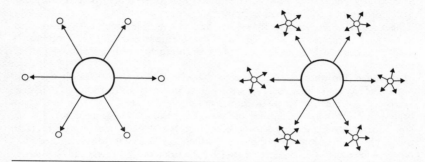

Fig. 1 Centre–periphery model   *Fig. 2* Proliferation of centres model

trainer of trainers. The central message includes not only the content of the innovation to be diffused, but a pre-established method for its diffusion. The primary centre now specialises in training, deployment, support, monitoring and management.'[15]

The proliferation of centres model has its counterpart in existing adult education structures in the shape of area and regional structures in both LEA and responsible body provision. In the former the central base may be a college of further education or an adult institute which controls programmes and resources in a range of outcentres within the framework of local authority budgets and regulations. Extramural departments and the WEA typically have a proliferation of centres in their district or region; in the latter there is a tradition of local lay control but within a broad framework of WEA policy and financing and with the professional guidance of a full-time educator.

The literacy programme is a good illustration of the proliferation of centres. Here the 'centres' are represented by the volunteer tutors often teaching within their own or their students' homes. These volunteers are subject to training by members of the central organisation in both the content and method of literacy teaching; the central organisation also provides continuous support and monitoring.

Schon maintains that there is a shift from the centre–periphery model of organisations to network structures functioning as learning systems. The concept of network was defined in the previous chapter and it is sufficient to remind ourselves that it 'is a set of elements related to one another through multiple interconnections'. The task of continuously building and maintaining networks of individuals and groups makes extensive demands on those responsible; the network agent must be all of the following.

Systems negotiator. . . . The vehicle by which others negotiate a difficult, isolated, rigid or fragmented system.

'Underground' manager. He maintains and operates informal, underground networks . . . across . . . agency lines – sometimes pursuing . . . functional goals that have little or nothing to do with the formal policies of the agencies involved.

Manoeuvrer. He operates on a 'project' basis, and is able through personal networks to persuade or coerce institutions to make the shifts required to realise a project that cuts across institutional lines . . .

Broker. . . . [He] connects buyers and sellers . . . and makes 'deals' if he is able to convince [them] that each has something the other wants. . . . He makes himself the 'node' connecting various strands which are otherwise disconnected . . .

Network manager. He oversees official networks of activities and elements, assuring the flow of information, the processes of referral, tracking and follow-up, and the provision of resources required for the network to operate.

Facilitator. He attempts to foster the development and interconnection of regional enterprises, each of which constitutes a variant of central themes of policy or function. His role is at once that of consultant, expediter, guide and connector.[16]

Essentially in such network roles the individual is a node linking strands of networks which, without his intervention, would be disconnected elements. To do this successfully he will need highly developed skills in establishing and maintaining personal relations.

It is fortunate that although Schon takes most of his own examples of learning systems and network roles from business and government his conceptual model has been used as a framework for two major adult education research programmes in England. These and other examples of experiment and practice will form the subject matter of a later chapter. Before this it is intended to apply the principles of job design enunciated earlier to the work of practitioners functioning in existing adult education institutions.

As with the principles of job design the relevance of the centre–periphery and network models to learning methodology is likely to have been spotted by the reader. For centre–periphery see the directive, teacher dominated style of teaching; in contrast the idea of a learning system has close links with a learning group where the teacher as controller is transformed into a resource person to be used by the group in any way appropriate to their collective development.

SUMMARY AND CONCLUSION

It is possible to approach the problem of system design from two directions. We can either start from scratch, creating an ideal system, or from where we are, that is change existing organisations in appropriate ways. These two approaches are here seen as being mutually supportive and both will therefore be explored.

An ideal system would create roles for people which took full account of their adult status. Existing organisations tend to frustrate adult needs for autonomy, challenge and the opportunity to learn, variety, etc. An ideal system would also be a learning system capable of continuing transformation. In contrast to the typical centre–periphery model of organisations this would be a network structure in which the key function would be that of network agent. Such a role is very demanding for the individual who must, therefore, have a support system to encourage and sustain him. In the particular case of adult education there must also be a supportive administrative framework in place of the typically restrictive range of rules and regulations.

There is no intention to develop the links between job design and learning strategies appropriate for adult students; that is a task for others. Nevertheless such an undertaking is consonant with building learning organisations.

REFERENCES

1. Advisory Council for Adult and Continuing Education (1979) *Towards Continuing Education*, Leicester.
2. Mee, G. and Wiltshire, H. (1978) *Structure and Performance in Adult Education*, Longman: London, pp. 40–1.
3. Ackoff, Russell L. (1974) *Redesigning the Future*, Wiley: New York, pp. 26–8.
4. *Ibid*. p. 26.
5. Schein, Edgar H. (1965) *Organisational Psychology*, Prentice-Hall: New Jersey. Ch. 4.
6. Maslow, A. H. ed (1954) *Motivation and Personality*, Harper-Row: New York; 2nd edn, 1970.
7. Argyris, C. (1957) *Personality and the Organisation*, Harper-Row: New York, and by the same author (1964) *Integrating the Individual and the Organisation*, Wiley-Interscience: New York.
8. McGregor, D. (1960) *The Human Side of Enterprise*, McGraw-Hill: New York.
9. Herzberg, F. *et al.* (1959) *The Motivation to Work*, 2nd edn Wiley-Interscience: New York.
10. Pollard, Harold R. (1978) *Further Developments in Management Thought*, Heinemann: London, Part **II**, presents a useful summary of some of these criticisms.
11. Emery, F. and Thorsrud, E. (1976) *Democracy at Work*, Martinus Nijhoff: Leiden.

12. Schon, Donald A. (1971) *Beyond the Stable State*, M. Temple-Smith: London; Penguin: Harmondsworth.
13. *Ibid*. p. 57.
14. *Ibid*. pp. 77, 80.
15. *Ibid*. p. 81.
16. *Ibid*. pp. 184–6.

CHAPTER FOUR

A comparative analysis of existing adult education organisations

There appears to be a consensus of opinion (ACACE, Fordham, Lovett, Russell) that much of the future educational provision for adults, whatever its label, will come from the existing major providers. As LEAs currently provide the vast majority of the programmes this chapter will focus attention in that area though reference will be made to other providers where appropriate. What follows draws extensively on the research findings of Mee and Wiltshire.[1]

In comparing adult education institutions the following characteristics will be used:

- formal linkages and accommodation
- staffing
- administrative environment.

FORMAL LINKAGES AND ACCOMMODATION

Within the broad administrative framework laid down by the employing authority adult educators can either find themselves operating their own programme independently of other services (i.e. a specialised service), or they can be part of the total provision of another institution primarily concerned with other functions, or they can be yoked to another service of more or less equal status.

There are three main types of linkage with other institutions or services. Adult education is given the right to use school premises without payment when they are not needed by the school. The school is the lender and adult education the borrower or, to put it in another way, the school is the host institution and adult education the lodger. The host may be willing or unwilling, and the linkage between host and lodger may be tight or loose. But lodgement of this kind clearly involves a more complex relationship than would a simple commercial transaction such as the hiring of a room.

A closer relationship is established when the lodger moves into and becomes part of the host institution; lodgement gives place to sharing. Adult education is seen not as a separate service but as one of the functions of the host institution which, as a result, may itself be redefined and enlarged. The most common hosts are colleges of further education and community schools; much less frequently the host is a leisure centre.

The third type of linkage occurs where adult education is not absorbed by, but is yoked with, a service which is seen as closely related to it, to form a new joint service. The usual partner is the youth service, and since the youth service like adult education is a scattered service with few substantial institutions of its own the two combine to form a new, specialised and separate adult-and-youth service. A more recent variant of this type has been the creation of a combined adult, youth and community service.

This idea of linkage is closely related to the degree of control which adult educators have over accommodation. There are three main possibilities here: the service may operate from premises which are its own in the sense that they are entirely under its own control (including hired premises); it may operate in borrowed premises, that is be in the position of using school premises usually in an evening (dual-use); lastly it may share the premises of the host institution which has adult education as one of its functions. These are not necessarily exclusive alternatives and some mixture is common. Some university extramural departments use all three arrangements, operating their own centres away from the university campus, holding some activities in university buildings and also making extensive use of borrowed accommodation.

Having one's own premises can be seen as adding significantly to the autonomy which the practitioner enjoys – it can markedly increase his elbow room. Alternatively premises of any kind, particularly if well appointed and attractive, can tie an adult education service: the building not only locates but helps determine the character of the service as being centralised and inward looking.

STAFFING

Within these different institutional settings are to be found a wide range of appointments in terms of title, status and the time commitment involved: tutor organiser, lecturer, community tutor, head of department, head of community studies, principal, head of centre, area organiser – these are some of a bewildering array of titles which reflect the different status of incumbents and, less certainly, differences in role. In terms of time allocated it is important to extend the customary distinction between full-time and part-time appointments, which inadequately reflects the situation. Effectively there are three categories, not two. A person may hold a full-time post in adult education; he may be a career adult educator. Alternatively he may hold a post in which he has a joint responsibility, part of his time being given to adult education and part to youth service, school teaching or vocational further education. He is a part-time adult educator holding a joint appointment. Finally he may earn his living by full-time employment in some other field altogether (perhaps school teaching or local government) but be employed as an adult educator in his spare time (as tutor or a head of centre). He is a spare-time adult educator.

The essential distinction between these three types of appointment is a quantitative one: the authority that makes a part-time appointment gives more man-hours to adult education than the authority that makes a spare-time appointment, but fewer man-hours than the authority that makes a full-time appointment. But there are likely also to be qualitative differences. The full-time adult educator will see himself as a professional and will think of his career in terms of adult education; he is, in every sense of the word, committed. The part-time adult educator is not so completely committed; he has two possible careers and can often switch from one to the other if it seems prudent to do so. The spare-time adult educator may seem the least committed of all, and so no doubt he generally is. But he may feel another kind of commitment: he may be doing this job in his leisure time because he likes doing it rather than simply for the financial reward; he may to some extent be a volunteer and this voluntary element may sometimes give his work a supererogatory zest and quality. This commitment is frequently expressed in a willingness to work for many more hours than he is paid.

There are not only a wide range of types of appointment but also of the number of appointments in any situation. A major adult centre may have as many as fifteen or twenty full and part-time professional organising staff plus a great many spare-time heads of centre and several hundred teachers (usually spare-time). In addition it will have full-time administrative, clerical and even technical appointments. At the other extreme, in some authorities a specialised service will consist of only a cadre of one or two full-time organisers for a whole county with the service being run by spare-time centre heads having, if they are fortunate, a few hours of clerical support per week. Similar contrasts exist in colleges of further education from a major department structure to a lone part-time tutor-organiser. In community schools one or two part-time staff seems to be the norm.

THE ADMINISTRATIVE ENVIRONMENT

Whatever the type of linkage or level of staffing adult educators work within a hierarchically administered environment of financing and of rules and regulations laid down by the local education authority. However different authorities exercise markedly different levels of control. Maximal control is exercised when the authority determines levels of student fees, enrolment and attendance minima, duration of courses, and so on and when grant is allocated (e.g. to tutor fees, clerical assistance, equipment) without any possibility of transfer. Minimal control is exercised when grant is given as a total sum. The institution is thus free to allocate this as it wishes and to set whatever levels of student fees, enrolment requirements, etc. it thinks desirable and (within this total expenditure) economically possible. There is an intermediate level of control in which the authority determines minimum levels of enrolment, etc. but allows these to be interpreted as applying to average levels in the institution as a whole, not separately to each course, class or activity.

Other factors than the framework of rules and regulations will determine the degree of autonomy of the practitioner. Control over accommodation has already been identified as an important factor; others would include his formal status, the degree of administrative and clerical support and his relationship to such lay bodies as student or members' councils.

JOB DESIGN IN ADULT EDUCATION

Using the principles of job design defined in Chapter 3 a comparison of the different kinds of adult education appointment will now be attempted by reference to the three characteristics identified, namely, formal linkages and accommodation, staffing and the administrative environment. The principles enunciated by Emery and Thorsrud (see p. 25) were concerned with autonomy, challenge and a chance to learn, variety, mutual support and respect, meaningfulness and a desirable future.

There can be no doubt that the adult educator operating within a specialised service, particularly if he is full time, has a greater measure of autonomy than any other category of practitioner. Not surprisingly he places great value and emphasis on the 'elbow room' that he has. He is physically remote from his employers and usually claims not to have a boss – he believes himself to be autonomous within the authority's regulatory framework. He is 'Mr Adult Education':

'I'm the boss, I run my own show.'
'We have the structure, we have the regulations, but by and large our employers allow us a lot of autonomy.'
'I expect officers of the authority to have faith in me and my team, to back that faith with resources and to give us near to total flexibility to adminster these resources, and I get it.'

The last quotation highlights a difference between the practitioner managing a large institute, having a 'team', and the principal of a centre with nothing more than clerical support; the latter sometimes complains of this lack of support and of feeling isolated:

'I am my own boss but we are cut off as though we existed on an island. . . . I need support and advice from the office.' 'I don't think that people who haven't worked in this way fully realise what a handicap it can be not only to work by yourself but to work at times when most people are free, to come out in the evening, to come out at weekends.'

In such circumstances autonomy can exact a price in terms of loss of mutual support and respect – there is no one handy to share your doubts or give advice in times of difficulty. Autonomy becomes isolation. However such observations seem to be related to the length of time in this kind of post; it is the relative newcomer to the role who sometimes experiences his freedom as uncertainty and consequently feels in need of support. Nevertheless, from time to time even the experienced practitioner is likely to be assailed by doubts and be in need of support.

In terms of autonomy there are very sharp contrasts between the experience of a practitioner operating in a specialised service and one working within a host institution such as a college of further education or community school. The first important point of difference is that in a host institution the boss is present in the organisation, not remote at county or city hall; the principal or headmaster is at the top of an organisational hierarchy within which the practitioner has to work. Additionally, sharing accommodation, ostensibly more favourable than a borrowing relationship, in practice seems typically to be conflict ridden: sharing tends to become competition for limited resources. This situation is exacerbated by the general lack of status of the adult service within the host institution. It is non-accredited, non-mandatory and often has to take budget cuts in excess of those required of the school or of vocational work. Thus there is not only less autonomy but a lack of mutual support and respect. In consequence in the further education college situation staff observed that 'adult education is last on the priority list' and that 'one begs often'. Similarly in the community school;

'If there is a clash of interest then we haven't got a snowball's chance in hell. Conflicts are reconciled in the interests of the school and there is very little day use.'
'There are clashes with school requirements in the evening and we often have to cancel a class.'
'There are conflicts over daytime use – it's bribery and corruption really – we're trying to move the school out of community use rooms.'

The last comment highlights a particular problem: where there is identifiable 'community use' accommodation the school, pressed for accommodation for its statutory work, has usually taken this over during the daytime. This situation may of course change considerably in some areas given the general decline in school populations.

Two factors tend to mitigate the limited autonomy and standing of adult education within a host institution: the formal status of the practitioner and the attitude of the principal or headmaster. Where there is departmental status or equivalent there is not only an adult educator operating at a senior level in the decision-making system but also a group of staff, however small, giving mutual support. This factor seems to have greater impact in colleges of further education than in community schools. Additionally in the former the existence of an adult department makes the principal aware that the service is important to the status and grading of the college;

'I'm certainly not having any nonsense about adult education being less important.'
'I determined that adult education should not be neglected; in other colleges it is often the runt of the litter.'

Where there is a department, principals also seem to adopt a supportive role external to the college:

'I can play a stronger line as the Principal of a major institution particularly with

the aid of my governing body, than they could do running solo and reporting direct to County Hall.'
'I must be seen as the flag-bearer of the adult education cause.'
'I defend the status and significance of AE wherever I can, at County Hall, in the Governors, in the press.'

Such comments often seem to reflect not only the interests of the college but also a personal commitment to adult education. This external political role was not, however, identified by community school heads who, in contrast, seemed to adopt a more passive role as counsellors or arbitrators in conflict situations; as one headmaster observed: 'Someone's got to blow the whistle when there's conflict over the use of facilities'.

The lack of status of adult education in general is probably most acutely experienced by many practitioners in the borrowing relationship. Whatever the organisational structure of the service there is almost always a need to borrow school premises for evening activities; frequently most of the programme of activities is located in schools. The problems encountered seem always to reflect the unfavourable attitudes of school staff at all levels:

'With caretakers you can't win . . . they tell me they are employed by the school and that they put up tables as an act of goodwill but they're damned if they're going to take them down.'
'Some of our worst enemies are school teachers . . . they do not see adult education as education.'
'Schools are our biggest problem where the heads can make it very difficult.'
'The school at times have put every obstacle they could in our way.'

There were also frequently quoted problems of storage: 'We live like moles'; 'My typical tutor is like a travelling tinker.' Several also pointed to the ambiguity of the policy about borrowing arrangements and would have welcomed a clarification of the situation; there was, however, little support for an edict from the Director of Education because of the possible backlash effect. Though officers at county hall often expressed awareness of the problem, appropriate action has not followed: 'The principals would like a statement from the Director about the dual use of premises . . . it concerns them greatly', one observed. Another commented that 'adult education is not accorded the respect due to it, the adult education chap is small fry, aggravating and upsetting what is going on in the school – there is a lack of appreciation and understanding at school and area level'.

It is to be anticipated that many of these problems of access to school accommodation would be solved in a community school system by moving from a borrowing to a sharing relationship. It has already been suggested that this is not so. Indeed the difficulties may be heightened because of the daily work contact with school staff; what in theory should be an advantage may become a marked disadvantage where school staff are unsympathetic to the work with adults. This is probably an inevitable consequence of operating a service with a small budget and few staff in 'partnership' with a hugely budgeted, mandatory school service with an extensive staff. In a conflict situation a headmaster (or for that matter some college principals) is faced with a political choice between a large school staff, with whom his professional sympathies lie, and a very few adult or community workers: in these circumstances it is to be expected that 'conflicts will be reconciled in the interests of the school'. When such conflicts are exacerbated by inadequate or non-existent budgetary arrangements for the increased use of school equipment and services the outcome is probably inevitable:

'There are inevitable problems of trying to operate a number of different services from one building using one set of facilities.'
'The school acquires nothing very tangible; our sewing machines are used by adults and we've engineered this now so that our dress-making class is taught by our needlecraft teacher, which helps; our typewriters are pounded cheerfully through most nights by adults.'
'I can only give community education the secretarial time that it needs if I steal it from the secretaries that are here because we are a school. And so the students at school are suffering. It's exactly the same in terms of the tremendous use that we make of the equipment. We don't get the machinery replaced any more quickly in the design workshops because it's used twice a day instead of once. But in the end it's the students at school who suffer because it's their equipment and we are here primarily for their compulsory education.'

As in a college of further education the lack of standing of adult education in a community school often produces problems of identity. One consequence of this feeling of vulnerability of being 'round the edge' is that community staff sometimes take on school duties over and above any formal expectation in their contract, as examinations or lettings officer, as fire officer or licencee; they like to be seen as having a role related to the whole school. Others use school teaching, either contractual or voluntary, as a means of establishing themselves. Though headmasters sometimes recognise the problems they cannot always see what could be done:

'The adult educator and the school staff have different life styles; time appears much less important in adult education, it's more leisurely.'
'It's a fairly isolated role; they work mainly at night and have little interrelationship with the 'day-shift'.'
'Our school staff haven't got it into their bones.'

Any role tension which community staff may feel as a result of their relatively low standing in the school is likely to be exacerbated by the often inadequate definition of the role by their employers. Comments like 'There isn't any coherent idea about the role', or 'We are trying very hard to define precisely what community education is', or 'It may be that the aim we are given of integrating with the school is an impossible one', identify the doubts which are frequently felt. Roughly one in three headmasters indicated an awareness of this role tension:

'We are inventing it as we go along.'
'Nobody has any idea what community school means.'
'The language is a real problem and shows the extent of our own confusion.'
'The community school or college seems to me at the moment to have such barriers of bad thinking in it that it's not going to get terribly far.'

The doubts which heads sometimes have about the concept clearly are visited on the community staff; not all share these doubts but among those that do the result may well be, as one adult educator claimed; 'I have never felt other than alienated.'

It can only be concluded that when operating inside host institutions, or when simply borrowing school premises, practitioners often face situations which markedly limit their autonomy and diminish their self-respect. At best there might be a high degree of tolerance but no real shared concern, and at worst an antagonistic school or college staff. It is difficult to see how they can experience their work as meaningful, in Emery and Thorsrud's terms, that is meaningfully contributing to social welfare, when those with whom they have to relate place so little value on what they do.

A conceptual framework within which to set the experience of adult educators working within such organisational environments has been provided by Burton R. Clark.[2] He suggests that in any organisation members will try to justify their objectives by reference to social values and that these values will be 'precarious' when they are undefined, when the position of functionaries is not fully legitimised and when they are unacceptable to a host population. Though he was writing of adult education in an American setting in the 1950s he offers an effective summary of the situation described above. Adult educators have usually found it difficult to define their objectives and to relate these effectively to underlying values; when they have to compete so directly for resources with other agencies whose values are legitimised by a host population the consequences are probably inevitable. The work does not appear meaningful to other educators or to the broader population. Local authorities often seem unsympathetic to the service's goals by making severe economies and by imposing a restrictive regulatory framework. Changing the name of the service to, for example, 'community' has made little, if any, difference to the standing of practitioners in an institutional setting.

Some LEAs even doubt whether it should be a publicly provided service. In consequence, in the 1970s practitioners have had to face economies and often major disruption of provision through budget cuts and fee increases. There has been a shift in emphasis in public debate, and action, towards a financially self-supporting service. For most adult educators this is a very positive indication of the low public standing of their work; for some it is a conspiracy, 'a back door method of closing the service down'.

Against such a background where is 'a desirable future' for practitioners? There is still no career ladder of the kind advocated by the Russell Report.[3] In general adult educators cannot see where they are going in career terms and many operating inside host institutions leave their options open and see their career progression in areas other than adult education.

The low priority typically accorded by LEAs to the service is also reflected in the degree of administrative and clerical support it receives; generally this is very inadequate, particularly in some specialised services. In consequence practitioners frequently complain of a clash between the administrative demands of the job and their desire to spend more time on the educational and developmental aspects of their work. It is partly the conflict which the Russell Report referred to between routine clerical duties and 'work relating to the nature and quality of the teaching and the supervision and development of staff which are fundamental to it':[4]

'I'm head of centre, caretaker, canteen assistant, anything that needs to be done at the time I do.'
'I spend half my time trying to find accommodation.'
'I'm just centre-bound with our staffing.'

In consequence of being 'centre-bound' practitioners often claim that not only are they unable to become involved with teachers and students but they are also prevented from getting out to research their own patch. There is no guarantee, of course, that if they were given all the support required they would spend the time gained on what can be conceived of as the leadership aspects of their role in contrast to routine administrative functions. The latter permit one to get 'wrapped in the embrace of the office' – on the other hand leadership can create problems and more work. As Burnham has observed, 'It is tempting to seek the quiet life, to avoid the dilemmas of leadership, by a retreat into "busywork".'[5] Such a response is likely to be reinforced by the feeling that many have that they are not adequately trained for the role.

Although some authorities have, at least in major centres, separated the two aspects of the role by appointing full-time administrative or clerical officers, the situation in general remains as it was described in the Russell Report; 'Over the years, many adult education principals have carried a quite unjustifiable load of routine clerical work which, ultimately, is undertaken at the expense of the educational supervision of the courses for which they are responsible.'[6] Thus any tendency adult educators may have to stress the administrative aspects of their work is frequently reinforced by the attitudes of their employers who clearly intend them to be desk-bound, to be form fillers and compliers with regulations governing fees and enrolments. This is not to suggest that such regulations are always complied with! Many practitioners bend the rules particularly in the frontline situation of a specialised institution; such a 'respectable deviousness' can provide enough elbow room for the creativity which is a feature of so much adult education work. Nevertheless regulations do create a lot of clerical work and are experienced as a serious discouragement to experiment and innovation.

There seems to be a general interest in and approval of averaging schemes which permit the head of centre some discretion; minimum enrolment numbers are an unnecessary and frustrating constraint. Net budgeting is another much talked about method of permitting a discretionary element at centre level but it is, as one senior officer remarked, 'double-edged', and does not always have the desired effect. 'It is both an instrument of greater flexibility and a way of preventing over-spending – I don't see people leaping in to transfer money from traditional work into newer ways of working; they are more anxious not to overspend than to exploit the opportunities it offers.' (The basic principle of net budgeting is that the adult educator is allowed to spend a net amount which is the difference between a total sum allocated and an estimated sum for fees paid by students.)

The clash between the administrative and leadership aspects of the role, though present, is complained of less in colleges of further education or community schools, probably because such institutions have a pool of administrative, clerical and technical resources which can be drawn on. On the other hand rules and regulations are probably more restrictive in their effects because of the presence of the boss within the organisation – it is likely to be more difficult to bend the rules.

No specific reference has so far been made to the work experience of the spare-time adult education organiser. Inevitably for him the constraints of too little, or even no, clerical support are exacerbated by the limited time he has for the work:

'The main responsibility is obviously administration. Most of the tasks are pretty menial; collecting money, issuing receipts, making sure registers are up to date, ordering equipment, that sort of thing. There's nothing difficult about the job but I find I'm sitting at my desk at home doing pay claims, etc. and it does take time.'

'There's no clerical assistance – except that my wife is an unpaid clerical assistant. A great deal of the work has to be done at home because people ring you up at home, and therefore I keep most of the records at home.'

These quotations do indicate a common response to the problem – the spare-time worker allocates much more time to the job than he is paid for and often involves his wife. When little or no clerical assistance is given he is bound to concentrate on the routine aspects of the role; clearly his employers expect nothing else.

In borrowing school accommodation the spare-timer has the same problems as anyone else. Though he will often operate within a specialised service his experience may be akin to that of community school or college of further education staff in that he is frequently employed in the school in which the 'evening centre' is located. Many clearly feel the conflict built in to such an arrangement, of knowing where their loyalties lie; others have solved this problem by working as an evening centre head in another school altogether. However, whether in their own or another school, most identify the difficulties of borrowing accommodation in the same terms as their colleagues in other kinds of institution; (among those that do not are to be found headmasters who operate as evening centre heads and must be tempted to keep evening provision down to a level which causes least disturbance to school activities):

'School demands in the evenings create rather a lot of problems.'
'I accept what the head will kindly give me.'
'It's a matter of great delicacy and diplomacy – of biting your tongue and grinning and bearing it.'
'The head is happy if we use one of his staff.'
'I wanted to offer pottery but the day-school staff were unco-operative . . . none of them would take it so it had to be dropped.'

Clearly, as in other situations, school staff frequently behave as if they have 'a divine right to the accommodation and equipment'; the same spare-time principal concluded that, 'If I want something I have to beg'.

SUMMARY AND CONCLUSION

Some readers may have reacted to this chapter with the observation, 'Not in my organisation!' It may be in some situations, through a happy coincidence of personalities and personal relationships, that many of the problems have been overcome; alternatively adult educators may have given so much ground that there is nothing left to fight about! It is clear, however, that many of the difficulties are structural, they are built into the organisation – they are larger than personalities and need to be designed out of the system. In general, therefore, it is maintained that the work experience of adult educators accords with the findings here reported.

Autonomy

Much the greater satisfaction here lies in working in a specialised institution. Practitioners operate in frontline situations and give themselves even more elbow-room by bending the rules and regulations to permit the development of activities which accord with their view of what constitutes an effective service. Their autonomy can be greatly enhanced by adequate administrative and clerical support and by having some teaching premises totally under their own control. There is a sharp contrast here with work experience inside a host institution where the boss is present in the organisation and the regulations are likely to be more difficult to circumvent.

Regardless of type of institution different employing authorities give a greater or lesser degree of discretion to adult educators in applying regulations and in allocating funds.

Mutual support and respect

There can be little doubt that in a host institution most adult educators are made to feel marginal to the enterprise. In trying to improve their standing they often take on extra duties related to the central function of the institution or use their teaching role to try to establish their respectability. They will feel less marginal if the work has departmental status and if they have a supportive boss who stresses the importance of their contribution. Their lower status is probably most effectively reflected in the difficulties experienced in sharing accommodation – they rarely win in competition with a stronger 'partner'.

Borrowing school premises presents major problems for all types of practitioner, whatever their organisational base. Their standing with others is frequently reflected in the obstructive attitude of headmasters, schoolteachers and caretakers. Local authority policy on dual-use, though evidence of goodwill, is often relatively ineffective. It is clearly not enough to say what should happen in situations in which adult educators borrow premises; the problem still remains of making the arrangements work in the face of the often conflicting needs of the school and its staff. It must be concluded that the hopes of the Russell Report have not been achieved in many authorities; teachers often still 'claim exclusive rights to publicly provided equipment' and many headteachers still 'protect the school building from being used as an adult institute'. The hoped for 'spirit of co-operation' is frequently not to be found and the difficulties are likely to prove insurmountable unless local authorities provide adequate caretaking and cleaning services and allow for 'faster depreciation' of plant and equipment.[7]

Meaningfulness

When those with whom you work tend to denigrate your efforts and your employers underfinance and undersupport the service it is hardly surprising that adult educators 'Sometimes have . . . doubts themselves – it isn't just that they see it in other people's eyes.' Their doubts are compounded when local authorities often regard the work as providing 'mere' recreation which does not merit public provision.

It should be added that these strictures apply to most local authorities – there are a few who give much greater support and approval to their adult education workers.

Desirable future

In the context described it is surprising that anyone ever stays long enough to find out whether there is a desirable future in the service. Adult educators must be either very thick-skinned or very resilient and committed to continue to work for many employing authorities. It is in the latter area that the answer lies – despite their many problems it would be difficult to find a more enthusiastic and committed group of workers.

In terms of career prospects the host institution, in which it is usually possible to keep one's options open, appears to be more favourable than a specialised service.

There is another undesirable feature of the work which has not been stressed so far. It is generally acknowledged that their sense of commitment usually causes adult educators, in whatever institutional setting, to work too hard and for too many hours. When in addition they have to work unsocial hours it is hardly surprising that many point to problems of being unable to separate their work from their home life and of marital strains. Not infrequently the work will intrude directly into the home with the adult educator's wife becoming a clerical assistant/telephonist, usually unpaid.

All kinds and all grades of adult educators are prone to overwork themselves. Though some employers seek to protect them from this tendency more are inclined to ignore it. The general failure to give adult educators sufficient clerical and other support obviously reduces the efficiency and enterprise of their educational work, but it also affects their personal and family life. Any notion of a desirable future has to take these things into account.

Challenge and variety

These factors in job satisfaction have not been specifically referred to. Nevertheless they are implicit in the adult educator's role. Within the constraints of the administrative demands of the job, the regulations and his own disposition, there are always new things to be attempted and challenges to be met. Indeed it is this aspect of their work which practitioners frequently identify as an important source of satisfaction despite the many frustrating obstacles to experiment and innovation.

In conclusion it must be acknowledged that there is much support in adult education organisations in the LEA sector for the hypothesis that there is a fundamental conflict between the needs of the adult worker and those of the organisation. The temptation may be to try to dispense with organisation altogether but this is too simplistic a response and must be resisted; existing organisations are here to stay – ways must be found of changing them.

REFERENCES

1. Unless otherwise indicated all quotations used in this chapter are from Ch. 8 of Mee, G. and Wiltshire, H. (1978) *Structure and Performance in Adult Education*, Longman: London.
2. Clark, Burton R. (1956) 'Organisational adaptation and precarious values: a case study', *American Sociological Review*, **21**, pp. 327–36.
3. Russell Report: Department of Education and Science (1973) *Adult Education: a Plan for Development*, HMSO: London.

4.   *Ibid*. para. 358.
5.   Burnham, Peter S. (1969) 'Role theory and educational administration', in Baron, G. and Taylor, W. (eds), *Educational Administration and the Social Sciences*, London, p. 90.
6.   Russell Report, para. 381.
7.   *Ibid*. para. 318, 343.

CHAPTER FIVE
Role theory and the adult educator

Throughout this book many potential conflicts in the adult educator's role are identified. As practitioners will continue to function within existing structures it is important to look at existing roles and their inherent conflicts. This can be effectively achieved within a framework of role theory which will not only permit some kind of classification of conflicts but possibly suggest ways of mitigating their effects.[1] As with much sociological writing role theory is jargon-ridden; here it is intended to avoid falling into that trap.

The concept of *role* has assumed great importance in organisation theory. An essential aspect of structure in organisations is the allocation of a particular position to each individual member. A position is a collection of rights and duties identified by a title, for example, principal of an adult centre, craft teacher, literacy organiser. The role which the holder of a position will be expected to perform will usually be expressed in a more or less detailed job description. This use of the concept role, to mean the expectations of one's employers, represents but one interpretation. Once in post, initial formal expectations will be reinforced or modified, not only by employers but also by colleagues, students, etc. It is useful to identify the many individuals and groups with whom one has work-related contact as the *role set*.

Role can also be viewed from the incumbent's position. Each individual brings to a job his own personality, his own qualities and needs. Therefore he will have a perception of the role as he would ideally like to perform it – ideally in the sense that it is in keeping with his own personal needs and also with his views, resulting from training and experience, of what an adult education service should be like. Some people are, for example, highly independent and would not welcome a tightly structured job description but would look for a large measure of flexibility in the role. Others, of a dependent nature, would find such flexibility threatening and would welcome a structured remit. We are here making a point similar to the earlier observation that it is not only organisations which have goals but also the individuals working within them; there is no guarantee of consensus.

There is a third possible use of the concept role: actual work behaviour. The way that an incumbent actually performs is likely to be a function of the interaction between the expectations which others have and his own conception of the role. Where the balance will lie will be determined by such factors as the degree of flexibility in the job description, how much an individual is able, or wishes to, create elbow room for himself, and his training and experience.

Role can therefore be used in the following three ways:

1. The expectations of others.
2. The individual's own perception.
3. Actual behaviour.

Using these three interpretations it is possible to organise the several possible causes of conflict in the job of the adult educator. Many of the illustrations will be drawn from the LEA field, though their relevance to other sectors will be apparent to practitioners.

There may obviously be a conflict between the formal expectations in a job and individual personality. This may become apparent at the interview stage, when presumably the particular individual will either withdraw or will not be selected. It is likely, however, that many working within adult education are ill-matched with the role. The not inconsiderable failure rate of part-time teachers, for example, may be due to the fact that many are not effectively matched with the demands of the role. A frequently missed opportunity to begin this process of trying to achieve a fit between the individual and the adult teaching role is the selection interview. Indeed there is often no prior contact at all. Where there is the practitioner is often ill-prepared, with little clear idea of what the interview is intended to achieve. If there is no clear picture of the role of adult teacher there will be no possibility of relating this to the needs, aspirations, skills and attitudes of the applicant, even if these can be uncovered.

When a person has been selected and is actually teaching the need to evaluate performance arises. Evaluation is potentially an explosive issue replete with possibilities for conflict. One problem is that although it should be an objective assessment of performance against known and understood criteria it is also, usually, an assessment of one person by another. (Ideally, in adult education terms, we should be aiming for self-evaluation. However, much still has to be done in the area of basic teaching skills training and given present financial stringency it is likely to be some time before we could contemplate the investment of resources to develop the necessary self-evaluation skills.) Therefore evaluation can easily upset personal relationships and the adult educator may be dissuaded from making the effort. It also presents other threats. Do I have the necessary skills? Do teachers accept that I have the expertise? The difficulty is expressed in such questions as 'Who can really understand the teaching of mathematics except another mathematics teacher?', and 'When did he last teach a class anyway?' In adult education the problem is partially eased because untrained teachers are employed and with these the organiser with teaching experience has some technical authority. Moreover, given that adult education is a different sort of activity to other teaching, and that an organiser has been trained in this specialism, this should enhance his authority even with the school teacher. Frequently, however, he is not specially qualified and his difficulties may be compounded if he is operating in a dual or multi-use building wherein he performs two roles which may conflict – during the day he is a member of a peer teaching group and in the evening has the task of administering an adult education centre in which a major source of teachers is likely to be the day school staff.

Given these difficulties it is probably not surprising that the criterion frequently used for judging the success or failure of a teacher is the ability to keep a viable class together, that is the maintenance of attendance at or above the minimum permitted by the regulations. This hopelessly inadequate measure does not contain the threats implicit in more complex and time-consuming evaluation processes. Indeed there may seem little point in either carefully matching the individual to the teaching role or in evaluating performance, given that there is no formal requirement to justify the conclusion that a particular teacher has 'failed'. There is no effective contract of employment for most part-time teachers and an individual is 'dismissed' by not being offered re-engagement the following session.

This is a morally indefensible position. There may be many reasons why a person experiences difficulties in the teaching role but all call for a supportive and not a dismissive response from the employer. Instead the tendency is often to shrug off the responsibility, leaving the teacher to cope with her sense of failure. Given that the adult education organiser has effectively created the problem, support in the form of counselling and training should be tried before rejection.

It has been implied that many practitioners avoid effective evaluation processes because they clash with their own needs – a desire not to create interpersonal conflict or doubts about their own capacity. The adult educator may justify his position by pointing to the administrative demands of the job which leave little time to be concerned about the quality of the teaching input. This may, however, often be a defence mechanism. If the adult educator can admit to a personal inadequacy in this aspect of the role then possible solutions suggest themselves. Training in the appropriate interpersonal and evaluation skills can be undertaken. Alternatively, certainly in larger establishments, it might be possible to delegate to someone better qualified. In some authorities experienced part-time teachers have been employed to act in a supportive role within particular subject areas. Essentially it has to be acknowledged that evaluation of performance cannot be allowed to go by default because the practitioner feels threatened by the process.

Other examples of possible conflict between personality and role have been identified in Chapter 4. The newcomer in a position may feel in need of a tighter role specification than is provided, though for many this may be a temporary settling-in phase. A more important and persistent example exists in community schools where the role of community tutor is usually ill-defined – 'There isn't any coherent idea about the role' reflects the typical situation. Incumbents often feel this as a threat which is reinforced by their often low status within the organisation. It may be that a generalised role description is appropriate to the particular stage of development of the community function. But if this is so then great care should be taken to match the individual to the role; a highly independent personality, welcoming and able to use flexibility in the role, has to be found. At present many incumbents appear to be ill-matched with the role. Further, the staff of a community school, employed in the tightly structured teaching role, have to understand the necessity for a loosely defined community function and give support to the individual trying to fulfil that function. At present the attitude is frequently, 'He never seems to be doing anything very much'; different work styles and hours make effective communication difficult. The community tutor is likely to respond to this personally threatening attitude by emphasising any teaching role he may have in the school and by taking on extra school duties.

One response to the need to achieve community consciousness has been to give all staff a small (10 per cent) time commitment to community work. This may solve the conflict problem but at the likely cost of neglect of the community function; if the latter lacks definition, if there is a task of discovery here, then there is a need for full-time, or at least substantial part-time involvement. Innovation is largely dependent on specialisation, on giving staff with the appropriate personality and skills the time to conduct the necessary search activities and to design appropriate responses to the needs they uncover.

An important source of role conflict is the difference which often exists between the employer's expectations and the adult educator's conception of the role. This is probably most clearly expressed in the clash between the administrative and leadership interpretations of the job which has already been examined in the previous chapter. The formal expectations expressed in rules and regulations, demands for statistical and other returns can be time consuming to the point where the adult educator has to neglect what he sees as his real function in educational terms. This clearly is a problem which creates a great deal of frustration for practitioners.

But the administrative/leadership conflict exists at another level. Administering and leading are both vital aspects of the adult education organiser's role. The organisation does have to be administered and maintained with its existing goals, structure, systems and regulations, and in doing this the organiser meets many of the expectations and needs of other members. Central office does expect to receive the appropriate claims for payment and teachers do expect to be paid the correct amount on time. The latter also expect that an amenable physical environment will be provided in which to teach and that advice and support will be available. Students do anticipate that any necessary equipment will be available to them and will function effectively and that rooms will be appropriately heated. In meeting these and other expectations the organiser will be experienced by others as a supportive and stabilising force. But the organisation also has to be led in new directions – new goals identified, new priorities established, new activities undertaken and new structures and procedures initiated. In adopting the leadership role the practitioner is likely to be experienced by others as a disruptive force and they are likely to resist his efforts at change. The likelihood that interpersonal conflict will be created, plus the extra effort involved, may cause this aspect of the role to be neglected. A great deal will depend on the personality of the organiser and on his skills in change management. Any deficiency in the latter area can probably be corrected through training. There will, nevertheless, be a strong temptation to concentrate on meeting members' administrative expectations rather than adopt the change-agent role with its attendant difficulties. It is undoubtedly less troublesome to get 'lost in the embrace of the office', to spend time checking registers and inventories and in submitting returns.

Another important source of role conflict will be the differing expectations of persons in the adult educator's role set. Thus central office may expect the closure of a class in which minimum attendance numbers are not maintained, whereas the expectation of teacher and students is that the activity is allowed to continue. The latter are unlikely to appreciate the distinction between an actual attendance of eight or nine and a requirement for a minimum of ten to be maintained. In schools and colleges the adult educator will be subject to conflicting pressures from his part-time teachers and their students on the one side and the full-time staff of teachers and caretakers of the institution on the other. The consequent difficulties have already been detailed. Anyone working in adult education is only too aware of the 'my room' or 'my kiln' syndrome and the difficulties this can create. The expectation is, do not create difficulties for me! For the organiser the situation can be very conflict ridden particularly if he is based inside the school or college. His days can be spent in placating full-time staff and the caretaker and finding alternative accommodation, and his evenings in appeasing his teachers and students.

Typically adult educators tend to be on the defensive, particularly in multipurpose institutions. The criteria which other educators tend to apply in assessing adult programmes have been generated within the very different secondary school or further education college sectors. By training and background most adult educators will have school and college teachers as an important reference group, a tendency reinforced by having to work with them in the same institution. In consequence they often feel guilty about traditional adult programmes. They are conscious of what significant others identify as the 'recreational' bias of adult work as reflected in the following breakdown of programmes in the LEA sector by category of subject.[2]

Category	Percentage of programmes
Craft and aesthetic skills	53·1
Physical skills	24·1
Cognitive and intellectual skills	16·7
Courses for disadvantages groups	6·1

The emphasis on craft and physical skills, usually more than 75 per cent of the total programme of institutions, is the focus of much criticism and a matter for concern among practitioners. In consequence each year they advertise their intention to run many courses in the more 'respectable' category of cognitive and intellectual skills, which they know from past experience are unlikely to recruit sufficient numbers. Thus in Nottinghamshire LEA provision in this category remained fairly constant over a period of twenty years (1955–56, 6.3 per cent; 1975–76, 8.2 per cent) despite continuing and sometimes strenuous efforts to expand in this area.[3] It should be noted that a particular determinant in Nottinghamshire has been the existence of a strongly developed university extramural and WEA programme which focuses almost wholly on the cognitive and intellectual field. There has been a tacit arrangement for an appropriate division of labour, and this has been reflected in LEA financial support for local responsible body provision. There would be little point in duplication.

A further consequence of what is seen as an unbalanced programme is that adult educators have tended to stress strongly their work for disadvantaged students, although this typically forms a very small part of the total programme. This area of work has also enabled some practitioners to mount a rather muted counterattack to the effect that, particularly in the case of illiterates, they are picking up those whom the school system has failed. This argument should be expressed more forcefully. With minimal resources adult educators in the LEA sector often seem to be expected to tackle all of the failings of the schools. Particularly with literacy programmes they have shown what can be achieved through commitment, imagination and voluntarism, with a relatively small injection of funds.

This analysis suggests that the practitioner in the LEA sector is placed in an almost intolerable situation as he experiences the conflicting expectations within his role set. He operates with a voluntary student body who will mostly only come to certain activities. His programme will therefore reflect their 'recreational' choices, a tendency reinforced by administrative expectations that a minimum number of students must be enrolled. On the other hand an important reference group, other educators, hold the resulting programmes in low esteem. Their judgement will matter to the practitioner having a similar training and background – indeed it will be of immediate and persistent concern if he has to work day by day with them in a multipurpose institution. One possible response to this disapproval would be to suggest to schoolteachers that they might try conducting the difficult, and personally threatening, mental exercise of imagining what the school curriculum would be like if the voluntary principle was used, that is if pupils were allowed to choose what subjects to study. Voluntarism in this sense would still fall short of the situation in adult education where students decide whether to attend at all; extending such a principle to schools would create extensive uemployment in the teaching profession. Schools would be very different institutions with a markedly different curriculum.

In this situation of conflicting expectations a joint appointment (part adult education, part school or college teaching) may be welcomed. In theory and in practice dual role demands are likely to produce conflict. However they also present an opportunity to meet the expectations of other educators for at least part of the time; adult educators can be seen to be teaching children, or say apprentices, in a structured situation, that is within a timetable and an appropriate subject discipline. Additionally, and this has become extremely important in the 1970s, a joint appointment enables the practitioner to keep his career options open. These advantages of the joint-appointment situation have to be set against the possibilities for conflict reflected in the following observations:

'It is only possible to do the adult education job properly.'
'I don't think it's fair to the children . . . I don't really give my mind fully to the school teaching job.'
'You can't mould the whole timetable around them, so therefore they just don't fit in.' (Community School principal referring to the difficulty of providing community tutors with an acceptable teaching commitment.)
'With the part-time teachers I'm the boss as it were but with the full-time College staff I'm just another lecturer with a particular responsibility . . . this is where I find most antagonism to my presence.' (A particular reference to the difficulties of teacher supervision.)[4]

A further role-set problem can be identified in outreach work. Differing expectations here can be linked with the difficulties presented by change situations. The outreach worker is essentially operating as a change agent, a function which colleagues concerned with more traditional work are likely to experience as a threat, particularly if funds for new work have to be found from within the existing budget. The head of an adult institute in such a situation has to be the arbitrator of differing expectations. The outreach worker expects funds to be found in order to respond to educational needs which are uncovered; such expectations are unlikely to be consonant with those of other colleagues.

Where there are such conflicting expectations

. . . the possibility exists of 'perceptual seduction' in that factors such as power, high status, propinquity, affiliation and the threat of sanctions, may 'persuade' the role incumbent to perceive one set of expectations as being more legitimate than another, irrespective of any objective importance or relevance. The administrator is constantly faced with the difficulty of assessing the legitimacy of expectations, and the relative weightings which are to be given to different sets of expectations, and he must be vigilant in guarding against perceptual distortion.[5]

Thus in a multipurpose institution an adult educator may accede to the stronger pressures of full-time staff who are likely to be supported in their attitudes by the headmaster or college principal. Again the outreach worker's interests may be neglected because of the more powerful, both in terms of number and formal status, representations of other staff.

How may the consequences of differing expectations be mitigated other than by allowing oneself to be perceptually seduced? One way, frequently adopted by adult educators, is to use the relative privacy of their frontline situation to ignore or bend administrative criteria in order to meet the expectations of students and teachers; at the same time they may also be giving expression to their own view of the role. This is a situation in which role behaviour may be at odds with the expectations of a particular group within the role-set without any undue strain on the incumbent. He plays down or ignores the expectations of some without them being aware of it. Where this is not possible then it may be that different individuals or groups in the role set may be unaware of their conflicting expectations and of the difficulties they are creating. If their actions are based on ignorance then telling them may effect a change in behaviour. Thus if there are demands from central office for frequent attendance at meetings which take up so much time that the expectations of teachers and other staff that the adult organiser be available for advice and counselling cannot be effectively met, telling central administrators of the difficulty may lead to less frequent demands. Again if administrative criteria are tending to prevent meeting the expectations of students then informing central office may effect changes which grant a larger discretionary element in the adult educator's role.

In an extramural department of a university, with its traditional emphasis on teaching and organisation, a member of staff may find himself at odds with some of his colleagues if he tries to meet intramural expectations for achievement in research and publication. Such conflict may be particularly acute for those who are physically based on the university campus while most of their colleagues function wholly extramurally in outcentres. It would be difficult to find in the university sector any instance in which the dichotomy between research and teaching is more explicit. Those who work extramurally are largely protected from internally generated criteria, insulated by their frontline situation. This is not to suggest that they do not do research, only that any conflict in the use of their time will be self-generated and not the result of pressures arising from an intra-university reference group. On the other hand adult educators based on campus may find themselves trying to cope with conflicting expectations generated by others. Where this situation exists it is my experience that explaining the difficulty to extramural colleagues can effect a change in the attitude of some.

If neither privacy in the role nor informing role-set members eases the conflict it may be necessary to achieve social support from others doing a similar job who experience comparable problems. Collective representation and action may be the only way of improving the situation. Here established collectives of practitioners can be invaluable as in ILEA (the Inner London Education Authority) with its associations of principals and of vice-principals. In Kent and Surrey adult educators also have an organised collective voice. Unfortunately these tend to be highly localised examples – in the main adult educators do not seem to be political animals. Increasingly if the experience of the 1970s is any guide, they will have to become so, if only to ensure that their case does not go by default.

This chapter has focused on intra-role conflict. In addition most adult educators experience inter-role conflict. We all play multiple roles in society as employee, marriage partner, parent, club member, etc. and there is a probability that these different roles may be in conflict from time to time. In adult education there can be no doubt that there is great potential for conflict between home and work roles. Working unsocial hours, often a three-session day, and not infrequently for more than five days a week, can create conflict in the parent and marriage partner roles. Collective political action to achieve better terms and conditions of employment and to exact greater clerical and administrative support is necessary but is not likely to provide a complete solution. The adult education service is not like teaching to 'O' or 'A' level or developing craft skills to Technician Education Council standards. There is no end product, no opportunity to say the job is done; the work is open-ended, success leads to yet more work and it is extremely hard for a committed practitioner to confine the process, to limit further development. His personal self may be seeking limits, but his professional self argues for pressing on into further search activities and new fields of endeavour.

SUMMARY

Role theory provides a very useful conceptual framework for achieving a better understanding of the adult educator's work experience and of the likely conflicts within it.

The concept role is taken to have three possible interpretations:

1. The expectations of others.
2. The individual's own perception.
3. Actual behaviour.

This typology is very suggestive of likely areas of conflict between:

(a) expectations and personality;
(b) expectations and the individual's own perception;
(c) differing expectations within the role set.

Expectations and personality

An example is provided by the need to evaluate teacher performance. It is suggested that because this is a potentially explosive process leading to interpersonal conflict, or because the adult educator feels the lack of appropriate skills, it is a frequently neglected area. Instead the wholly inadequate criterion of teaching success is often simply the ability to hold a viable class together. Practitioners who experience conflict in this area of their work should seek appropriate skills training or alternatively delegate to someone who is competent.

A further example of role/personality conflict exists in community schools where there is often little understanding of the community role. In consequence incumbents experience a high degree of uncertainty which is exacerbated by the low esteem in which school colleagues hold the role.

Expectations and the individual's own perception

The clearest example of conflict in this area is between the administrative and leadership interpretations of the role. Adult educators are often frustrated in their desire to develop their programme by the expectations of employers expressed in restrictive regulations. But conflict here exists at another level, linking closely with role/personality conflict. To adminster effectively is to be experienced by other organisational members as a stabilising supportive force making for feelings of security. Attempts at change are likely to produce disruption for others as well as for the change agent. For this reason practitioners may choose to avoid the change role. Again training would be relevant, in this instance in change-management skills.

Differing expectations in the role set

Administrative criteria, expressing the employer's expectations, are likely to conflict with the wishes of teachers and students. Additionally the interests of the latter are often likely to be in conflict with those of the staff of the host institutions.

Further conflict can arise because the demands of voluntary students for a popular programme mean that the programme is unlikely to satisfy the expectations of other educators. It is suggested that the conflicting expectations of students, reinforced by administrative criteria on the one hand and of educators on the other, place the adult educator in an almost impossible position.

Outreach work would also appear to present role conflict possibilities for the head of an adult institution.

Where there are differing expectations within the role set there are dangers of perceptual seduction when trying to achieve a balance between them. In attempting to achieve a more positive balance there would appear to be three possible approaches:

- use the privacy of a frontline situation to ignore some expectations.
- tell role–set members of the difficulties they are creating – they may possibly be acting in ignorance
- seek social support in order to achieve collective representation of the difficulties and, if necessary, action to effect changes.

REFERENCES

1. Burnham (see Ref. 5, Ch. 4) is recommended to those readers interested in developing a better understanding of role theory as applied to educational organisations. The framework for this chapter is taken from that source.
2. Mee, G. and Wiltshire, H. (1978) *Structure and Performance in Adult Education*, Longman: London, p. 32.
3. Hughes, J. T. (1979) 'The provision of non–vocational adult education by the Nottinghamshire Education Authority 1944 to 1975', M.Phil., *University of Nottingham*, dissertation. There was a temporary increase to 13 per cent in 1970/71.
4. Mee and Wiltshire, Chap. 8.
5. Burnham, p. 82.

CHAPTER SIX

Changing existing organisations: the management of change

There is broad agreement between Lovett and Fordham *et al.*, that the activities generated at Liverpool and Southampton could not have occurred within existing administrative and organisational structures. Established attitudes, rules about fees and numbers and the institutional base represented insurmountable barriers. Fordham *et al.*, therefore see the future development of 'non-formal education . . . probably in the main outside of existing institutional structures and traditions'.[1] Lovett, however, suggests that: 'The present system can, as most adult educators are aware, be manipulated and made use of if there is a sense of commitment on the part of those concerned. Rules and regulations can be stretched . . .'.[2] The Mee and Wiltshire findings indicate that they are indeed stretched – a 'respectable deviousness' is manifested at field level. Officers at county or city hall are sometimes aware of what is happening but show no desire to constrain efforts to break new ground by strictly enforcing the rules. Indeed this would be difficult given the privacy of the frontline situation in which practitioners often work.

This chapter will proceed on the assumption that the present system is amenable to change, though the process is likely to take considerably more time than, for example, the Southampton team had at its disposal; even they, however, do acknowledge that they were beginning to influence local providers towards the end of the project.

CREATING A CLIMATE FOR CHANGE

It was suggested in Chapter 4 that there are certain undesirable features of existing adult education organisations which could be designed out of them; in this way their capacity for change could be markedly improved.

Primarily each adult education structure must be given the maximum autonomy consistent with accountability to its paymaster. Here, for example, some local authorities have shown greater imagination than others permitting discretion at local centre level, within the limits of a total budget, to set whatever fees, enrolment requirements etc. are thought to be appropriate. Another essential is that within host institutions, the adult service must have at least departmental status – it must be seen to be on par with other areas of work in the organisation. Such formal status is no guarantee of equal treatment, but without it the situation can be very difficult.

Adult educators in whatever setting must be free to perform the educational and development aspects of their role. Therefore adequate clerical and administrative support must be given. Although this is likely to require the injection of more resources into the service it is possible to identify areas where existing resources could be used more effectively, where volunteer labour might be used and where other than educational funds might be tapped. The tradition of voluntarism is well established inside the WEA and in extramural work, and more recently has become a feature of some LEA work, with the use of volunteer tutors in the literacy programme, the involvement of part-time teachers in such activities as enrolment and counselling, and student committee members helping to administer coffee bars and organise other social activities. This trend should be nurtured and its further development possibilities analysed; voluntarism is in keeping with the best traditions of adult education.

Questions need to be asked about the present use of existing resources. For example, in the LEA sector is there any real justification for paying educationalists, usually schoolteachers, to do the spare-time organising role in the many satellite centres detached from parent institutions? Among the arguments used to support the arrangement are that it is an educational role and also an effective training for the full-time workers of the future. In effect it is neither of these. The spare-time organiser is typically a relatively highly paid clerical worker without training in the appropriate skills; such an introduction to the nature of work within the service is hardly adequate preparation for the role of *adult educator*. Resources sufficient to permit the appointment of a further full-time, or substantial part-time worker(s) might be released by employing clerical assistants as spare-time organisers. A personable individual with the appropriate clerical and book-keeping skills is likely to be more effective than an educationalist who is not allowed by the nature of the work and the pressures involved to exercise his skills.

It will be argued that it is useful to have a teacher organising the programme of evening activities in a school; he will give the service some status in the organisation and therefore ease the problems of dual-use. This is one of the myths of the service. It has already been shown that the spare-timer working in the school in which he is also employed full time is subject to conflicting pressures which are unlikely to be resolved in the interests of adult education. How can it be otherwise given that he has to 'live' with his full-time teacher colleagues? Working in another school may depersonalise the conflicts but does not remove them. Headmasters often do the evening centre organiser role themselves or encourage a senior member of staff to do so; in this way the school can be protected from the worst consequences of dual use.

On balance, therefore, it can probably be concluded that using school staff in this way is likely to work against the interests of the adult service, it might overcome some of the problems of dual use but only because adult education gives ground in conflict situations. The good intentions of local authorities on the dual use of school premises would be closer to realisation if certain administrative arrangements were introduced; they will cost money but must follow from any serious intent to use more intensively and effectively what are, after all, community buildings and equipment. Thus they must ensure that there are adequate caretaking and cleaning services to cover a three-session day (as already exists in colleges of further education), and a six or seven day week. They must also allow for the inevitably faster depreciation of plant and equipment. Given the typical inadequacy of present arrangements it is hardly surprising that school staff become defensive, even obstructive, when faced by the consequence of dual use. *Behaviour is structurally determined and the causes can, therefore, be designed out of the system*. There will always be some who adopt a 'my room' stance, but this would no longer have the justification of being in defence of the interests of schoolchildren; it will be seen for what it would be, naked self-interest.

It is not only in the LEA sector that inadequate clerical and adminstrative support is given. University adult departments are also offenders here and in consequence highly paid academic staff are often engaged in relatively routine tasks. It is an inadequate defence to point to the difficulties of the present restrictions on funding new appointments for the problem has persisted for a long period through the good times and the bad. Although in the LEAs there is the same problem of inadequate support, that sector does have something to teach university departments and the WEA also, in the use of its organising staff. A resident tutor (i.e. a member of the teaching staff resident in a particular area having responsibility for organising a programme of classes for that area) of an extramural department has, in addition to his organising role, a fairly extensive teaching programme. In contrast a local authority usually expects a full-time organising commitment, an acknowledgement that the service can be developed (provided, that is, that the adult educator is given adequate support and funding). In its use of resident tutors an extramural department seems to be saying that it is in business to do what it already does; certainly there is little time for development of a fundamental kind. Some tutor organisers have responded to this situation by working impossibly long hours in order to develop work, particularly with new groups of people, or to further a community project or to support new tutors. As in the LEA sector employers have tacitly accepted this situation, they have abused the commitment and goodwill of practitioners. Although no statistics are available I suspect that one consequence of this is a high rate of marital stress and breakdown among adult educators.

Another structural aspect of adult education institutions which needs to be critically assessed is the formalised arrangements for 'community' participation in the work of colleges, community schools, extramural departments and the WEA. Such arrangements take the form of councils, advisory committees, etc. the membership of which tends to reflect a narrow spectrum of interests. Thus, though relevant to existing provision, they are likely to be an effective barrier to broader community involvement; they tend to harden existing organisational boundaries. Some practitioners may allow themselves to be seduced into thinking that through such councils or committees they are effectively in touch with the community – they may be an important psychological crutch in a situation in which the service affords them little standing in a host institution or with their employers. Others who are not seduced in this way are aware of the danger inherent in the committees and confine the members to, for example, fund-raising and organising social events; programme planning they believe is a matter for professional judgement not an opportunity for serving vested interests.

One response in some areas has been to widen the representation on such committees. Thus they might include not only staff, students and members, but also voluntary organisations, local politicians, the caring services and the trade unions. Such wider representation would not only broaden considerably the range of community involvement, of access to social networks, but would add political muscle to the service;

even some presently constituted, narrowly representative, committees have proved useful in favourably influencing local authorities contemplating economies in the service.

MANAGING CHANGE

Granting maximum autonomy to practitioners, freeing them to concentrate on their educational and development functions and examining and improving existing arrangements for community involvement, will all facilitate change. But altering the framework in these ways, though necessary, only helps to create an environment more favourable to change; they are not a guarantee that change will occur. It is also necessary to have organisational members with the appropriate change management skills. In looking at the conflict between the administrative and leadership aspects of the adult educator's role it was suggested that training in such skills would be appropriate. Here it is intended to indicate a possible framework within which to approach such skills training.

The literature on planned change in organisations and its management is vast. Even within education, as Baldridge and Deal have noted, there is 'an enormous body of literature which continues to grow at a staggering rate'.[3] No attempt will be made here to survey this extensive literature. Only a limited selection will be presented which has been found to be particularly useful by adult educators studying on Diploma and Master's courses.

Baldridge and Deal maintain that three types of knowledge are necessary to an understanding of change processes in organisations:

1. Knowledge of the organisation and its sub-systems.
2. Knowledge of change strategies.
3. Knowledge of actual change situations (i.e. case studies or practical experience).[4]

The structure of adult education organisations has already been analysed and recommendations made for changes in certain sub-systems, for example, the administrative and communications sub-systems. Change may be attempted in any one sub-system but it has to be understood that it is likely to affect other aspects of the organisation and these consequent repercussions have to be anticipated and responded to if change is to be successful. Thus, for example, the change of technology occasioned by an inadequately resourced literacy programme, from a taught group to one-to-one teaching by volunteers, was bound to raise difficulties for the control and communication sub-systems. Socialising volunteers through training programmes was only a partial answer. The operational problems of controlling and containing the frontline volunteer tutor/student relationship has probably led to the growing tendency to revert to the more easily influenced taught group situation. A further example is provided by the introduction of net budgeting. Though primarily intended to enable central administration to control expenditure net budgeting was also thought to give greater discretion to adult educators in planning their programmes and in catering for minority interests. What seems to have occurred, particularly in the period of budget cuts, is that the tendency to provide popular classes has been reinforced as practitioners have tried to increase income from student fees.

These and other case studies reflecting the interdependence between sub-systems need to be written up in order that we can learn from them. At present in adult education such material is scarce.

The implication so far is that change in organisations is likely to be a complex process. With this in mind Baldridge and Deal have produced a useful list of criteria to assist those planning change to evaluate their strategies:

1. There must be a serious assessment of needs.
2. The proposed changes must be relevant to the history of the organisation.
3. The proposed changes must take the environment into account.
4. Major changes must affect both organisational structure and individual attitudes.
5. Changes must be directed at manipulable factors.
6. Changes must be politically and economically feasible.
7. Changes must effectively solve the diagnosed problem. [5]

In relation to the particular criteria Baldridge and Deal identify certain problems and questions. Assessing needs objectively is unlikely to be easy for the 'captured' change agent – being part of a system makes it difficult to stand back and analyse it. Moreover the easily visible problem may only be the tip of the 'iceberg'; indeed it may not be the problem at all. What does the environment need and what will it support?; here is the now familiar open system interacting with other systems in its environment. Changing the structure by, for example, introducing participatory decision making is likely to encourage a change of attitude but it has to be acknowledged that attitudes, like goals and the environment, are likely to be resistant to change. More manipulable factors are structure (e.g. appointing an outreach worker), personnel practices (e.g. promotion) and technology (e.g. the introduction of one–to–one, mixed craft or team teaching).

Whatever change is contemplated it is essential to gauge the likely opposition and to ensure that the necessary resources are available. Finally all change efforts must be treated as opportunities for learning. If the problem is not solved, the need not met, then it is necessary to find out why and to learn for the future. In this learning process the Baldridge and Deal criteria are invaluable because the answer is almost certainly to be found within one or more of their categories.

Developing strategies requires an understanding of the forces which make for resistance to change. A very useful starting point here is Goodwin Watson's observation that,

All of the forces which contribute to stability in personality or in social systems can be perceived as resisting change. From the standpoint of an ambitious and energetic change agent these energies are seen as obstructions. From a broader and more inclusive perspective the tendencies to achieve, to preserve, and to return to equilibrium are most salutary. They permit the duration of character, intelligent action, institutions, civilization and culture.[6]

In attempting change it is therefore important to assume resistance in both individuals and social systems; such resistance is purposive for both. The distinction is an arbitrary separation because 'the forces of the social system operate within the individuals and those attributed to separate personalities combine to constitute systemic forces'.[7]

Watson suggests that resistance in persons is due to many factors, several of which clearly overlap: 1. homeostasis (the tendency to return to a stable state); 2. habit; 3. primacy ('The way in which an organism first successfully copes with a situation sets a pattern which is usually persistent.'); 4. selective perception and retention (existing attitudes determine response to new ideas – thus teachers or managers when exposed to new philosophies rarely change their actual behaviour); 5. dependence ('All human beings begin life dependent upon adults who incorporate ways of behaving that were established before the newcomer arrived on the scene. . . . The inevitable outcome is conservative'); 6. superego ('a powerful agent serving tradition'); 7. self-distrust ('Who am I to suggest changes in what the wisdom of the past has established?'); 8. insecurity and regression ('the tendency to seek security in the past').[8]

Our purpose here is not to analyse Watson's views critically but to suggest a broad range of forces which tend to make for resistance to change in individuals and, further, to identify similar forces at work in organisations. Thus he maintains, for example, that 'norms in social

65

systems correspond to habits in individuals'. Change threatens customary behaviour which organisational members expect of each other; such norms are difficult to change because 'norms make it possible for members of a system to work together. Each knows what he may expect of the other. The abnormal or anomic is disruptive.'[9] Change is also likely to affect vested interests within the organisation; groups or individuals may believe that their economic or status interests are at stake.

These are some of the links which Watson attempts to establish between resistance in individuals and in social systems. Fortunately for the reader interested in developing his change management skills Watson summarises his conclusions in a very useful checklist which includes several ideas linked closely with Baldridge and Deal's criteria for assessing change management strategies. Watson sees this list not as laws but as being 'based on generalisations which are usually true and likely to be pertinent'.

Who brings the change?
1. Resistance will be less if administrators, teachers, board members and community leaders feel that the project is their own – not one devised and operated by outsiders.
2. Resistance will be less if the project clearly has wholehearted support from top officials of the system.

What kind of change?
3. Resistance will be less if participants see the change as reducing rather than increasing their present burdens.
4. Resistance will be less if the project accords with values and ideals which have long been acknowledged by participants.
5. Resistance will be less if the program offers the kind of *new* experience which interests participants.
6. Resistance will be less if participants feel that their autonomy and their security are not threatened.

Procedures in instituting change
7. Resistance will be less if participants have joined in diagnostic efforts leading them to agree on what the basic problem is and to feel its importance.
8. Resistance will be less if the project is adopted by consensual group decision.
9. Resistance will be reduced if proponents are able to empathize with opponents; to recognise valid objections; and to take steps to relieve unnecessary fears.
10. Resistance will be reduced if it is recognized that innovations are likely to be misunderstood and misinterpreted, and if provision is made for feedback of perceptions of the project and for further clarification as needed.
11. Resistance will be reduced if participants experience acceptance, support, trust, and confidence in their relations with one another.
12. Resistance will be reduced if the project is kept open to revision and reconsideration if experience indicates that changes would be desirable.[10]

The resistance to change model makes an important contribution to our understanding of the management of change in organisations. It recognises that unless resistance is overcome a change effort is almost certainly doomed to failure. In order to do this Watson identifies several strategies with which adult educators are likely to be in sympathy, for example, power equalisation between management and other organisational members, consensual group decision-making and the need for empathy and support. Thus the checklist presents an approach to change management which is likely to be invaluable given that resistance is anticipated. However, it has an inherent weakness. The implicit focus is on *initial* resistance to change; only the last recommendation is explicitly concerned with resistance which might arise *after* the introduction of a particular change, that is as a result of actual experience of the new situation. This limited focus has been criticised by N. Gross *et al.*, in an insightful case study of innovation in American schools: 'One of our basic reservations about the 'resistance to change' explanation was that it ignores the whole question of barriers that may be encountered by members of organisations in their efforts to carry out innovations.'[11]

These *implementation* barriers may produce resistance at a later stage even among those organisational members who were positively oriented towards the *introduction* of change. Therefore Gross has advanced his 'Leadership Obstacle Course (LOC) Theory'[12] which is based on the following assumptions; (once again the overlap with Baldridge and Deal will be apparent).

1. If there is resistance to a *proposed* change this must be overcome before there is any possibility of *implementation*.
2. Five conditions are necessary to successful implementation:
   (i) organisational members must have a clear understanding of the proposal;
   (ii) they must possess the appropriate skills and capabilities;
   (iii) the necessary resources must be available;
   (iv) existing organisational arrangements must be compatible with the innovation;
   (v) members must be motivated to spend the required time and effort.
3. It is management's responsibility to ensure that these five conditions are met.

In this model the responsibility of the change manager is explicit – he has the task of overcoming these implementation barriers. In order to assist others to adopt a changed role he must have a clear understanding of the innovation and a firm commitment to it. Without this how is it possible to instil confidence in others? Members' (and his own) needs for training have to be identified and the resources necessary for success made available. Effective feedback mechanisms must be established to ensure that any difficulties experienced are quickly identified and responded to. Existing organisational systems and rules and regulations must be examined to assess their compatibility with the proposed innovation and any necessary changes effected. It is the responsibility of the change manager to remove these and any other 'organisationally rooted ' barriers.

In applying the LOC theory to a series of case studies of educational change Gross and Herriot[13] have identified limitations in the model which have caused them to advance an elaborated version. They maintain that it could be improved if its 'time line' was extended to include the *exploration* and *strategic planning* stages of the process. It is also too inward-looking and does not take account of circumstances *external* to the organisation. Additionally it excludes some *internal* obstacles and does not make formal provision for barriers which reappear and for monitoring and feedback mechanisms. Finally, it excludes the political responsibilities of the change manager's role.

This elaborated model is probably the most sophisticated development in educational organisation change theory, and adult educators would find a detailed study rewarding. Earlier it was suggested that in adult education there is a scarcity of case study material in organisational change; practitioners could help to remedy this by writing such studies, utilising the elaborated Gross and Herriot model as a framework for analysis. In order to encourage this process both their model, and an associated table of leadership tasks have been reproduced in full. Some may react to the Gross and Herriot model by suggesting that it is based implicitly on the idea of management control of change. This may be so, but the essential argument of this chapter is that there is a need for adult educators working inside organisations to develop change management skills and to accept the *responsibility* for achieving effective change, whatever the process by which the need for change is recognised and wherever the balance of power lies in that process.

SUMMARY AND CONCLUSION

A basic assumption of this book is that existing adult education organisations can be changed. Attempts to effect such change would be greatly assisted if each adult education organisation was given the maximum autonomy consistent with accountability, together with adequate clerical and administrative support, and if existing formalised arrangements for 'community' participation in decision–making were made more representative. However, altering organisations in such ways will only help to create an environment more favourable to change, it is not a guarantee that change will occur.

It is of little use freeing the practitioner to perform a change management role if he lacks the appropriate skills. A framework to assist the acquirement of such skills has been presented. It is a first essential that adult educators know how organisations and their sub-systems function – a purpose which earlier chapters were intended to serve. Case studies in organisational change also have to be researched. Such studies could be provided by practitioners utilising the models which have been presented. Many current situations could be analysed, for example the outreach programme in ILEA, local literacy programmes, the development of campus schools in Sheffield and of urban community schools in Coventry. Attempts have been made to analyse these and other examples of change but not, so far as I am aware, within a framework of organisational change models.

The adult educator also requires a knowledge of change strategies. To this end it was felt to be useful to provide busy practitioners with relevant checklists the use of which should facilitate the development of appropriate strategies. Overcoming resistance to change is one area where skills and strategies have to be developed. Additionally it is necessary to have an understanding of both the likely barriers to implementing change in organisations and of the change manager's responsibility for overcoming such obstacles.

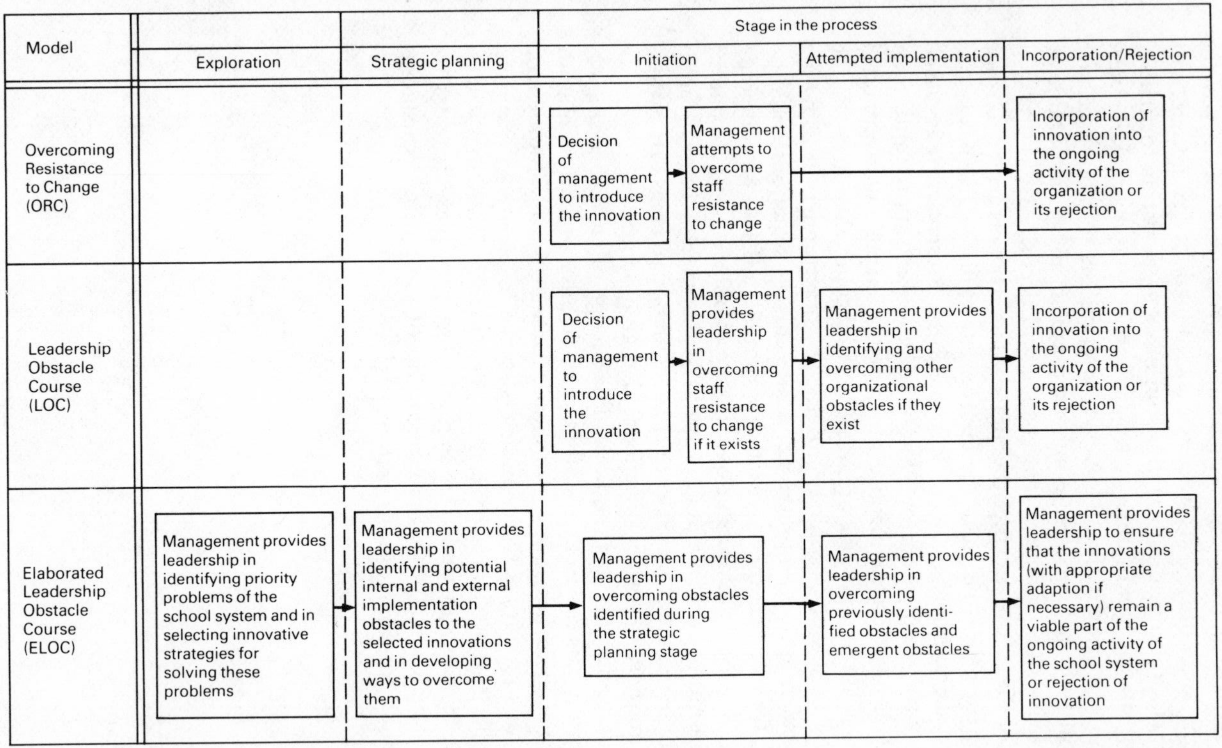

Fig. 3 Three models of planned educational change: The Overcoming Resistance to Change (ORC) model, the Leadership Obstacle Course (LOC) model, and the Elaborated Leadership Obstacle Course (ELOC) model

		Stage in the process		
Exploration	Strategic planning	Initiation	Attempted implementation	Incorporation/Rejection
Provide leadership in identifying: 1. The major current problems of the school system 2. The priority in which these problems need to be addressed 3. The range of possible solutions to priority problems in view of the "political" situation 4. The obstacles within the school system that can block particular solutions to priority problems 5. The strengths within the school system that may facilitate particular solutions to priority problems 6. The resources from beyond the school system that may be available to implement particular solutions to priority problems 7. The most promising solution, i.e., the innovation to be attempted	Provide leadership in: 1. Identifying potential obstacles to the implementation of the innovation 2. Identifying potential facilitators to the implementation of the innovation in this school system 3. Developing a realistic strategy for minimizing each obstacle and maximizing each facilitator of this innovation in this school system 4. Obtaining the financial resources necessary to implement this innovation in this school system 5. Specifying internal and external political considerations that can have a major bearing on the innovation and developing strategies to cope with them	Provide leadership in overcoming obstacles identified during the strategic planning stage such as: 1. Staff lacks the necessary motivation 2. Staff lacks the necessary technical knowledge 3. Staff lacks the necessary interpersonal skills **4. Staff lacks the necessary instructional resources** 5. Dysfunctional organizational arrangements within the school system 6. Conflicts between different groups within the school system 7. Conflicts between the school system and its community 8. Conflicts between the school system and its external funding agency 9. Cultural values within the community in conflict with the idea of change **10. Lack of consensus about, or support for, the change effort**	Provide leadership in overcoming previously identified obstacles and emergent obstacles such as: 1. Misunderstandings about the objectives of the innovation 2. Misunderstandings about the procedures of the innovation 3. Resignation of key school system personnel 4. Turnover in the membership of the school board 5. Turnover in the staff of the external funding agency 6. Role overload on the part of teachers or administrators 7. Delays in receipt of necessary instructional materials 8. Serious political problems confronting the change effort	Provide leadership in ensuring that the innovation remains a viable part of the ongoing activity of the school system by: 1. Obtaining views about the innovation from teachers 2. Obtaining views about the innovation from students 3. Obtaining views about the innovation from parents 4. Obtaining objective evidence on the degree to which the innovation is achieving its intended objectives 5. Obtaining objective evidence on the financial costs of continuing the innovation 6. Assessing the benefits of the innovation in the light of its costs 7. Considering the desirability of continuing the innovation without modification 8. Considering the desirability of continuing the innovation with modification 9. Considering the desirability of abandoning the innovation altogether

Some basic leadership tasks of key school system officials in change efforts under the Expanded Leadership Obstacle Course (ELOC) model

REFERENCES

1. Fordham, P., Poulton, G. and Randle, R. (1979) *Learning Networks in Adult Education*, Routledge: London, p. 207.
2. Lovett, Tom (1975) *Adult Education, Community Development and the Working Class*, Ward Lock: London, p. 144.
3. Baldridge, J. V. and Deal, T. E. (1975) *Managing Change in Educational Organizations*, McCutchan: Berkeley, p. 2.
4. *Ibid.* pp. 1–2.
5. *Ibid.* pp. 14–18.
6. Watson, G. (1970) in Bennis, W. G., *et al.* (eds), *The Planning of Change*, Holt, Rinehart and Winston: London, p. 488.
7. *Ibid.* p. 489.
8. *Ibid.* pp. 489–93.
9. *Ibid.* p. 493.
10. *Ibid.* pp. 496–7.
11. Gross, N. *et al.*, (1971) *Implementing Organizational Innovations*, Basic: New York, p. 196.
12. Herriot, R. E. and Gross, N. (eds) (1979) *The Dynamics of Planned Educational Change*, McCutchan: Berkeley, pp. 34–8.
13. *Ibid.* chap. 14.

CHAPTER SEVEN

Experiments in the organisation of adult education

In the Introduction it was suggested that practice in adult education is not infrequently ahead of theory, pointing the way forward. It is possible to link some of this practice with recent findings of organisation theorists researching in other settings in an attempt to move towards an alternative theory of adult education organisation.

In reporting on their research into schools in the United States, Baldridge and Deal have maintained that 'any social organisation seeking innovation must make itself vulnerable by opening channels of communication and influence to its environment'. They therefore recommend that: 'Part of an environmental outreach programme should include special intermediary positions between an organisation and its community and the development of strong boundary roles. Top administrators of any organisation always fill a boundary role, but other links are needed.'[1]

It has already been suggested that any adult education organiser performs a boundary role. Additionally, the service is replete with examples of 'special intermediary' appointments – outreach worker, organiser for literacy, community education worker – whose function is to develop 'strong boundary roles', to create new social networks for the service. They open up channels between the organisation and the environment with a view to identifying needs to which organisational resources might appropriately be allocated. In other words they function by bringing messages back to the central organisation where response capacity exists; they identify an opportunity for innovation and help to create a climate for its implementation.

Beyond the implementation stage it is likely that the resources of the organisation will be needed to sustain and develop the innovation for, as Baldridge and Deal further suggest, 'decentralisation may promote innovation but, once initiated, innovation spreads and is sustained by a centralised and administratively complex management'.[2] The development of literacy programmes in the 1970s exemplifies this process. Tutors or tutor organisers for literacy, often part-time, were appointed by local authorities within the context of the national campaign to combat the problem. They functioned by developing a range of social networks with, for example, caring agencies, local radio, the press and industry, in order to identify potential students. In order to respond to these students the literacy organiser had to rely mainly on the resources of the local authority adult education service to provide a base of operation, for tutors, to train volunteer tutors, and so on. Once the demand for literacy programmes was uncovered and grew, part-time organisers sometimes became full-timers and more literacy staff were appointed. What had begun as a simple administrative arrangement of an extra appointment(s) very quickly became a complex structure involving hundreds or even thousands of students, hundreds of volunteer tutors, training staff and the maintenance of a range of social networks.

Detaching adult educators from their organisation tends to overcome the suspicions which adults entertain towards educational institutions. Such thinking lay behind a recent attempt by the Institute of Continuing Education, Londonderry, to reach working–class women in the town who did not use the adult education service. 'The uneasy relationship between the institutions and the public can be relieved by the employment of tutors, released from the confines of the institution, to liaise between the academics and the public at a neighbourhood level.'[3] To this end a part-time tutor organiser was employed 'whose sole responsibility was to create study/action groups in the community offering an alternative, but equally satisfying educational experience'. The need for organisational support was recognised from the beginning; '. . . she had access to fellow tutors, the library, printing services and audio-visual equipment – all essential back-up services in a venture which was to meet many different demands'. The tutor could also draw on a resource centre, chosen as a base for the work, whose aim was to make resources and information available to local people. This centre was run by trained volunteers.

In addition to resources it was also recognised that, 'as an innovator, the tutor required constant support and guidance'. This was provided by a member of the Institute staff. These two themes, the need for a resource base and for psychological support are recurrent themes in the literature on organisational outreach. A further study in the comparable field of youth work, is relevant here. John Leigh, in his work on youth and leisure in a Derbyshire town, observed that, 'the literature about detached youth work in this country suggests that it is a job demanding expertise in a variety of social work skills and that the worker is frequently subject to very considerable stress'.[4] He maintained that this stress element is not always effectively understood. The possibility of failure, and certainly of rebuff, is ever-present. The detached worker might, 'emerge from this situation with his enthusiasm destroyed and with a sense of personal failure. Morally, it seemed indefensible to put anyone in a working situation of this sort.'[5]

Whatever relevant skills the detached worker brings to the role, because he is in an exposed situation, he will tend to be drawn into areas in which he lacks competence. This vulnerability is exacerbated because, 'the detached worker does not have a door he can close to shut out those with whom he does not want to work. He can be selective in that he tries to involve himself with some groups and individuals rather than with others . . . but the limits within which this selectivity operates are totally different from those possible in a structured working situation.'[6] Therefore Leigh advocated training and the support of a team, or at least the support of a competent individual.

Such arguments are highly relevant in the context of the observations in Chapter 3 on the nature of job satisfaction. In the outreach worker situation there is too much elbow room, a difficulty in identifying a meaningful role, no readily available way of evaluating achievement and the dangers of a lack of mutual support and respect. When faced with the inevitable feelings of inadequacy or even failure in the role the worker is likely to see the central organisation as a haven, to identify with its expectations of him and therefore to become less effective in the outreach function.

Specifically in the adult education context the ILEA appointments of 'outreach workers' probably represent the most highly developed example of relevant practice. Does experience there bear out the findings of the more limited experiments referred to?

An ILEA report of 1973 showed, not surprisingly, that the London Adult Education Institutes were serving mainly the better educated sections of society. This middle-class bias, a matter for concern and debate wherever practitioners meet, is a criticism frequently directed at the service. In the context of such districts as Bethnal Green, Deptford, Peckham or Lambeth, it was felt to be particularly inappropriate. Concern led to action. In an attempt to broaden the basis of recruitment 'outreach workers' were appointed to many of the major institutes. The general expectations of outreach workers are reflected in the following extract from the job particulars for one such appointment though it should be noted that specific remits would vary from institute to institute.

The post is for a second Community Education Worker with the general responsibility of extending the Institute's work in the neighbourhood. The person appointed would be required to strengthen existing relationships and sustain a number of on-going projects in addition to establishing new contacts with local voluntary and statutory groups. An important role of the community education worker is to research and identify learning needs in the area for the policy making process and to experiment in conjunction with the Institute team, with ways of meeting these needs, especially among people not normally attracted to Adult Education.

He/she should be able to work sensitively and sympathetically with a variety of people and in a variety of situations and respond by initiating classes which might be of an informal, unstructured and experimental nature. At the same time he/she would have careful regard for accepted educational standards and would be especially concerned to encourage recognition for the full potential of existing adult and further educational provisions.[7]

It should be noted that the outreach staff were joining well-endowed adult organisations; there is a strong resource base. The typical London Institute has many full-time staff in both the organising and the teaching functions. There is a separation of the educational and administrative roles through the appointment of senior administrative officers. There are also full-time clerical and technical staff. Educational activities are organised not only within the main centre but in numerous out-centres – sixty to seventy is not uncommon – not only in schools but also in settlements, high rise blocks of flats, in fact almost any kind of building which can be pressed into service. Each institute has a board of governors and an academic board. Therefore, in adult education terms, these are very well resourced organisations and, therefore, in the British setting atypical.

The concern here is not to evaluate the effectiveness of outreach appointments in such a context; indeed it would not be an easy task even to set up the necessary criteria, which are still a matter for debate within the London service itself. Our interest is centred on the experiences of the workers and on the responses to these experiences. Nevertheless it should be acknowledged that the achievements, though inevitably uneven, have been considerable in such institutions as Frobisher, Bethnal Green, South Lambeth, Central Wandsworth, and other London boroughs.

ILEA has a tradition not only of experiment but of attempting to evaluate its innovations. It is fortunate that at the time of writing the local inspectorate, the staff of the institutes and the outreach workers themselves are engaged in just such an evaluative exercise, and that their observations have been made available to the author. There is always a feeling of excitement about such a process and it is a rare privilege to be given a sight of it.

The ILEA experience not only reinforces the need for access to a resource base and for support but also adds considerably to our understanding of the difficulties encountered and of ways of overcoming them. Thus the outreach workers' feelings of isolation seem to be strong: 'The experience of many outreach workers, working in isolation in an institute bewildered by their presence . . . suggests . . . that it would be pragmatic to attach two outreach workers . . . to each adult education institute.'[8] Having a 'team' of two workers will provide some support, but there are other recommendations too for 'regular information seminars' with elected members and for 'firm guidelines' for the work. They would also like their work to be judged by a wider range of criteria than is normally applied in the service, and there is a call for greater understanding from colleagues: 'We would strongly urge that institute-based and branch-staff meetings become the stated policy of the Authority, and staff are paid for attendances. In this way, tutors will become less isolated and the outreach worker can become an organic part of the Institute.'

The last quotation indicates that there are difficulties in relating to their resource base – the institute. As one of the first outreach workers to be appointed Michael Newman has identified, in a highly readable account, the possible root of these difficulties.

Certainly to those principals who were content to see out their few remaining years of service providing a standard programme of hobbies and interests the first few outreach workers must have seemed a rum, and threatening bunch . . . We operated with extraordinary freedom. Although we had been appointed to each institute below the principal and vice-principal, no one really knew what we were meant to do . . . nor often enough where we were.[9]

Experience of course will vary. Some institutes will prove to be more responsive resource banks than others depending to a great extent on the attitudes of senior staff. Obviously the work generated by a community education approach can be seen as being in competition with subject oriented departments. In the situation of nil growth which has persisted in the service it is probably inevitable that such new activities will be experienced as a threat to established provision, particularly as they are usually more expensive than traditional work.

The sympathy and co-operation of institute staff cannot therefore be assumed, there are built-in possibilities for conflict over the use of resources which may not be resolved in the interests of the outreach workers. When it is noted that the appointments are made at the relatively junior level of Lecturer Grade II the likely outcome of any conflict is forecastable. The problems are likely, however, to be considerably eased by a supportive Principal who protects the outreach work by giving to it a guaranteed allocation of tutor hours from within the total institute budget.

The administrative framework, which in ILEA is much more supportive than most, is nevertheless experienced as being unsympathetic, and the outreach workers would like to see changes made. Regulations governing fees and staff/student ratios and the complexity and delay of enrolment procedures are all seen as constraining factors. Suggestions for change vary from abolishing fees altogether to modifying fee and attendance regulations to take account of such factors as irregular attendance due to shiftwork or domestic commitments. There is also the observation, frequently expressed in all aspects of adult education, that the administrative load increases with the amount of educational activity generated. The more you succeed the less time you have to build on that success. Therefore, as in adult education, generally, if outreach workers are to continue to use their time in development work it is necessary to give the appropriate administrative support.

The outreach function involves a whole range of skills necessary to building inter-agency co-operation in the community. Whether working within the education service or with agencies from other sectors, co-operation, and hopefully co-ordination, is not easy to achieve:

Much of our work has involved us with other sectors of the service, i.e. Nursery Schools and Further Education, Learning Resources, Youth Service, etc. We have found that the restrictions which define and separate each branch of the service stunt the growth of integrated Community Education (e.g. age ranges, time of operation, qualifications of staff). Similar difficulties occur when working with other agencies, both statutory and voluntary. However, field workers are increasingly involved in such integrated work, as exemplified in home visiting schemes, parent involvement in primary and secondary schools and introduction to employment. Once again, we feel that the solution to such restrictions lies with the establishment of regular forums for consultations, to complement the work of consultative committees. These forums could initiate information days, working parties, advice surgeries and 'Education Shops'. An Education Service based upon a series of jealously guarded territories can only become more and more irrelevant to communities who are increasingly providing education for themselves on their own terms, because the Authority has failed them.[10]

The examples of practical efforts at changing institutional boundaries by using outreach workers to develop new areas of work can be set within Schon's conceptual framework of a *learning system*. Indeed two further comparable examples of practice use his model. These examples, both adult education action research projects, have been reported by Tom Lovett[11] and Paul Fordham *et al.*,[12] respectively. Lovett, a WEA employee, conducted his research as a member of the Liverpool Educational Priority Area team and Fordham *et al* were members of the Extra-Mural Department of Southampton University when they directed the New Communities Project in Leigh Park, Havant. These will be compared in order to move towards an alternative theoretical model for adult education systems. Both would accept as a starting point in such an undertaking not organisations but Freire's dictum that, 'The point of departure . . . lies in men themselves. But since men do not exist apart from the world, apart from reality, the movement must begin with the men–world relationship . . . with men in the "here and now", which constitutes the situation within which they are submerged, from which they emerge, and in which they intervene.'[13]

Both projects therefore adopted a learning stance acknowledging that men's needs 'are neither objective nor readily discernable';[14] 'only time and personal involvement brought the detailed knowledge' required.[15] Building and maintaining social networks were essential to such learning. Lovett identifies the approach as one which reverses the centre–periphery model.[16] Similarly for Fordham *et al*, 'a matrix of independent learning groups and networks', offered, 'a positive and dynamic alternative to a number of separate professionally dominated and controlled services . . . '.[17] The key function is that of network agent. The complex nature of this role as described by Schon is reflected in both examples; '. . . researchers, action men, teachers, publicists, organisers, catalysts'.[18] Lovett lists a range of tasks in a community adult education network – network agent, resources agent, educational guide, teacher.[19] In his attempts to assist groups in a network to learn we are told that a professional worker needs certain qualities:[20] 'Above all, he must subscribe to the view that a major objective of his work is to help establish networks of people with knowledge, access to resources and sufficient confidence to act in concert to transform their environment, direct their own learning and widen their horizons.' Additionally he must be,

Able to relate expertise and knowledge to the social experience and particular needs of people;

Accessible and capable of listening deeply and seriously;

Prepared to eschew control or colonisation;

Prepared for people to take things into their own hands and to say in which direction they want to go;

Prepared to learn from his own interaction with learning groups and then to influence his colleagues and the agency that employs him;
Capable of improvisation in the field of administration and be prepared to help divert resources to assist learning groups.

Most would be found wanting in the face of such demands and it is not surprising, 'that the problems of role definition and selection of tasks was formidable'.[21] Those operating in such an environment are likely to experience the sensation of 'passing through zones of uncertainty . . . of being at sea, of being lost, of confronting more information than [they] can handle'.[22] Our earlier observations on job design argued for an appropriate balance between autonomy and variety; in the tasks associated with the role of network agent there would appear to be far more elbow-room than most could tolerate without considerable support. When this is compounded by periods of 'failure and rebuff' it is to be expected that the reports of both action research projects would conclude that there was a need for a strong support team sharing a common philosophy.

Support teams provide not only a crutch for the individual but can also contribute to continuity of both networks and innovations. Fordham *et al* stress that non-formal work 'will remain sporadic and experimental unless the right support systems can be developed';[23] unfortunately we learn that there were only limited opportunities to develop this idea during the life of the project. Support systems may also help to overcome the problem of discontinuity encountered, for example, when a member of the Southampton team left; we are told that his replacement could not simply 'inherit' the same networks and therefore the work in question closed down.[24]

The need for support groups has been recognised in some London institutes. Jim Anders, Principal of the Frobisher Institute, has identified both the need for such support and the demands which the creation and maintenance of the appropriate networks make on the outreach worker.

Wherever possible a support group of people sharing our concern for the 'problem' is formed. This group advises on content and where possible harmonises the educational input with the complementary services provided by other agencies and assists in monitoring the work. To facilitate such support, our outreach workers have had to maintain productive liaison with a wide range of agencies including: Further Education, Youth Service, Schools, Careers Service, Community Relations Officers, Social Services, Area Health Authority, Community Settlements, Councils of Voluntary Services, Manpower Services Commission, Training Services Agency, Department of Employment and Department of Health and Social Security, Churches Associations supporting work with the mentally handicapped, mentally ill, battered wives, single parents, physically handicapped, the elderly, addicts, conservationists, etc., etc. Even two Community Education Workers are over-stretched, just by this one task.[25]

Experience in ILEA also lends support to a further conclusion of both the Southampton and Liverpool projects, that evaluation on the basis of customary criteria would have ensured failure. All echo the conclusion of the Russell Report:

Insistence upon regular times of meeting, the routines of enrolment and registration of attendance, minimum numbers, the charging of fees in advance (or at all), and formal class teaching will often destroy any chance of successful educational penetration into these sectors of the population. Whatever the providing body, it must be imaginative and flexible in approach, it must recognise that progress will often be slow and difficult to evaluate, it must be prepared to support its staff in discouragements and false starts, and it must allow for the inevitable expense.[26]

The consequences of restrictive administrative frameworks have already been examined. Here it is sufficient to note that the work in Liverpool, Southampton, Londonderry, ILEA and in the literacy programme would not have been possible within such a setting. In Liverpool the attitude to fees reflected the underlying philosophy:

It was also accepted that the education provided in the EPA should be seen as a social service and offered free with the LEA reimbursing the WEA for class fees . . .

It was a matter of positive discrimination resting on the belief that since the existing adult provision was subsidised for those who had already benefited most from education, there was a social obligation to reverse this process and encourage greater participation by those who benefited least by education but needed it most.[27]

For Fordham *et al.,*

. . . the administrative constraints of the institutional system produce a negative influence not only on potential participants but also on . . . staff. Rules that govern availability of class, subjects to be taught, costs and fees and length of courses or the use of premises provide a hidden agenda for teachers and students alike.[28]

Given the need for experimentation, the likelihood of failure, the waiving of fees and the relaxation of regulations, we should not be surprised to learn that the work in both cities was much more expensive than traditional adult education. Therefore any intention to widen the provision, to reach out to new publics and to meet their needs, will have to be supported by additional resources. One possibility would be to divert existing resources which, to some extent, has been a feature of ILEA's programme of outreach. The problem is that the typically small budgets for adult education offer little opportunity to divert resources without destroying the existing service. The alternatives are to divert resources from other sectors of the education service, to find alternative sources of funding in other public sectors such as health and social services and employment, and to approach industry.

SUMMARY

Organisational theorists argue that organisations seeking to innovate should open up channels of communication to their environment. To this end they should establish special intermediary positions with a remit to develop strong boundary roles and extensive social networks.

There are many examples of such roles in current adult education practice. Experience in these consistently identifies certain essential features which need to be taken full cognisance of in appointments of this kind.

1. The role makes heavy and complex demands on incumbents; a wide range of skills is required which few are likely to possess.
2. A strong support team is required, the possibility of failure, plus the difficulty of identifying an appropriate way of working, calls for continuing psychological support.
3. An effective resource base is required if innovations are to be sustained and developed.
4. There is a need for an appropriate administrative environment which provides not only adequate clerical support but also waives traditional evaluative criteria as expressed in rules and regulations about fees and numbers.

Finally it has to be acknowledged that by comparison with traditional adult education classes such outreach work is relatively costly to mount and develop.

REFERENCES

1. Baldridge, J. V. and Deal, T. E. (1975) *Managing Change in Educational Organizations*, McCutchan: Berkeley, pp. 171, 73.
2. *Ibid*. p. 164.
3. Lovett, T. and Mackay, L. (1978) 'Community based study groups – a Northern Ireland case study', *Adult Education*, **51** (No. 1), pp. 22–9.

4. Leigh, J. (1971) *Young People and Leisure*, Routledge: London, p. 129.
5. *Ibid*. p. 130.
6. *Ibid*.
7. I am grateful to Maurice Cook, Inspector for Further and Higher Education (ILEA), for making the job description available and also for much advice.
8. This and the following quotations on the outreach workers' experience are taken from 'Initiatives for Restructuring Community Education', an unpublished paper drawn up by a group of ILEA outreach workers. I am grateful for their permission to quote from what is a very insightful paper.
9. Newman, M. (1979) *The Poor Cousin*, Allen & Unwin: London, pp. 115–16. This is an extremely interesting personal account of the work in ILEA. The author identifies both the background to the appointment of outreach workers and also provides a useful summary of the different kinds of initiatives taken by individual workers (Ch. 15).
10. See Note 8. (*ibid.*)
11. Lovett, Tom (1975) *Adult Education Community Development and the Working Class*, Ward Lock: London.
12. Fordham, P., Poulton, G. and Randle, R. (1979) *Learning Networks in Adult Education*, Routledge: London.
13. Freire, Paulo, (1972) *Pedagogy of the Oppressed*, Penguin: Harmondsworth, p. 57.
14. Fordham, *et al*., p. 36.
15. Lovett, (1975) p. 44.
16. *Ibid*. p. 129.
17. Fordham *et al*., p. 202.
18. *Ibid*. p. 33.
19. Lovett (1975), pp. 132–6.
20. Fordham *et al*., 201–2.
21. *Ibid*. p. 33.
22. Schon, Donald A. (1971) *Beyond the Stable State*, M. Temple-Smith: London; Penguin: Harmondsworth, p. 12.
23. Fordham, *et al*., p. 222.
24. *Ibid*. p. 146.
25. Anders, J. (1979) 'The Range of the Outreach Worker in Adult Education', conference paper delivered at University of Southampton. I am grateful to Jim Anders for permission to quote and for the time he has so willingly spent in explaining to me the imaginative work of the Frobisher Institute.
26. Russell Report: Department of Education and Science (1973) *Adult Education: a Plan for Development*, HMSO: London, para. 284.
27. Lovett (1975), p. 126.
28. Fordham, *et al*., p. 203.

CHAPTER EIGHT
Structuring for fundamental change

The time is right for fundamental change in adult education. Both society and the individuals and groups who comprise it are faced with profound, probably traumatic, changes. Without a compensating and rapid development of a comprehensive education service for adults massive social and personal disruption is inevitable; such a service will not prevent disruption but it can at least mitigate its effects. It is in this context that the continuing reduction in adult provision in the 1970s has to be set. If the responsibility for developing a comprehensive service is left, as at present, largely in the hands of the LEAs the future looks bleak. However the attack on the service may yet be seen to have made an important contribution to its salvation. It has mobilised public opinion in support of adult education; it has led to an acceleration and strengthening of the debate on future needs and, probably of more immediate importance, it has created surplus human resource capacity in that some practitioners find themselves underemployed.

What is now needed is central government initiative to take advantage of this situation of mobilised opinion, informed debate and underused expertise. With relatively minor government funding, in the context of total educational, health, social services and employment spending, a foundation for a new, comprehensive education service for adults could be laid. Such a government initiative could show returns in a few years – the price is small compared with the costs of inertia. If the problems are not tackled by a positive, constructive, educational response then the resulting costs will have to be met by the social and health services and by the forces of law and order.

The changes which are necessary are only going to be possible within a restructured system. It has already been noted, however, that social systems are resistant to change. It will be remembered that Schon sees existing organisations as 'memorials to old problems', thus expressing a widely accepted belief that bureaucratically structured systems are not innovative, or at best are very slow to change. This characteristic, some writers argue, will ensure the demise of traditional organisational structures in a world in which there is not only rapid change but an accelerating rate of change. As the need for innovation accelerates organisations demonstrate an increasing incapacity to respond.

So long as a society is relatively stable and unchanging, the problems it presents to men tend to be routine and predictable. Organisations in such an environment can be relatively permanent. But when change is accelerated, more and more novel first-time problems arise, and traditional forms of organisation prove inadequate to the new conditions. They can no longer cope. [1]

In this context many writers have identified a need for more flexible, loosely structured, organic, even transient systems which are set up in response to a particular problem and then discarded. These views cannot be accepted without question. Organisations can and do change, sometimes in quite significant ways given some relatively limited structural adjustments and the existence of committed and able change managers. Nevertheless, there is much for adult educators to learn from those who urge us to look 'beyond bureaucracy', particularly as existing structures are regarded with suspicion by most adults. It is neither possible nor even desirable, however, that there should be an adult education service without organisation in the traditional sense, only that such structures need a major reorganisation. Organisations may be to some extent ineffectual but they are by no means irrelevant.

It has been suggested earlier that some factors such as attitudes and goals are highly resistant to change. The structural changes which were advocated, plus the development of change management skills, are unlikely to be effective in making changes in such areas. Nevertheless fundamental changes are essential if a fully comprehensive education service for adults is to be developed. Success here is likely to depend on building flexible new structures which relate to established organisations in appropriate ways.

Donald Schon provides an effective starting point in the attempt to provide a conceptual framework in the search for a mode of reorganising. He develops the resistance to change model into the very fertile idea of the 'dynamic conservatism' of social systems. It is not just that organisations have simply a negative tendency to resist change but that they demonstrate a very positive and active 'tendency to fight to remain the same'. The following extract sets out clearly the dynamic relationship between what Watson identified as the comparable forces making for resistance in both individuals and social systems:

What is more, dynamic conservatism is by no means always attributable to the stupidity of individuals within social systems, although their stupidity is frequently invoked by those seeking to introduce change. But why, then, should systems fail to reflect the intelligence of their members? The power of social systems over individuals becomes understandable, I think, only if we see that social systems provide for their members not only sources of livelihood, protection against outside threat and the promise of economic security, but a framework of theory, values and related technology which enables individuals to make sense of their lives. Threats to the social system threaten this framework.

A social system does not move smoothly from one state of its culture to another. In processes of social transformation, societies move from a relatively stable state through a zone of disruption to a new zone of relative stability. Something old must come apart in order for something new to come together. But for individuals within the system, there is no clear grasp of the next stable state – only a clear picture of the one to be lost. Hence, the coming apart carries uncertainty and anguish for the members of the system, since it puts at risk the basis for self-identity that the system had provided.

It does not matter, then, if change may be seen in retrospect to have been harmless or even beneficial. Before the fact, the threat of disruption plunges individuals into an uncertainty more intolerable than any damage to vested interest. The self then puts its own conservative energies at the service of the system's conservation.[2]

Members need their organisation not only for the economic security it brings but because it gives order and identity to their lives. Change threatens them with uncertainty and puts at risk the basis of their self–identity, thus their own conservative energies serve to perpetuate the system.

When the need for change cannot be resisted then the system responds by making 'the *least change* capable of neutralising or meeting the intrusive process. . . . Nominalistic or token changes are of this order: an old department may be renamed in the terms of the rhetoric of change.'[3] Such observations appear very pertinent in the context of recent attempts to give new labels to what continues to be a largely traditional adult education service. Changing the label does not of itself change the provision, it may only serve to confuse practitioners.

How then is fundamental change to be effected in organisations? Schon holds strongly to the view that it does not occur through the conventional process of 'analysis of objectives, examination of alternatives, and selection of the most promising routes to change'. Such an approach, he argues, assumes that rational plans can be sold to others or will somehow implement themselves. Therefore he advocates 'invasion and insurgency', terms which 'recognise the warlike and disruptive character of change'.[4]

Anyone who has worked in any of the organisations within the adult education service is likely to hear echoes of his own experience in Schon's views. The capacity for the service to look the same, ten, twenty or even thirty years on is acknowledged by many, if not most, practitioners. Many attempts have been made to identify new objectives and ways of achieving them but with no or too little consequent change. Possibly the only important exception to this general rule is the national literacy campaign, but this required central government initiative and funding. The impetus for change came from outside the system and new resources were found and new systems created to make the change possible. It is significant here that a fundamental change in technology, the use of volunteers in a one-to-one tutorial capacity, working outside of education centres, seems to be now on the retreat; the traditional technology of teacher and class is reasserting itself in many areas.

There are dangers in generalisation. The Mee and Wiltshire research did uncover significant exceptions where quite fundamental changes in the adult education service had occurred, where individuals were functioning outside the traditional boundaries. But it is important to note that these exceptions were typically to be found in specialised centres, functioning as frontline systems where the commitment and energy of a particular individual(s) could find expression given the measure of autonomy found in such situations;[5] initiatives were taken which were difficult to supervise from county or city hall.

Such idiosyncratic findings do not affect the general picture of an adult education service with a remarkable ability to stand still or to change at a leisurely pace and in a minimal way. Even the much discussed changes resulting largely from the Russell Report's identification of disadvantaged groups in society rarely account for more than a small part of an institution's work some years after publication of the Report. The fact that adult educators talk a great deal about such a typically small proportion of their work is because it has social approval and therefore offers a defence mechanism against those who hold the traditional provision in low esteem.

Therefore Schon has much to tell those interested in changing the service, to making it relevant to the whole range of educational needs of adults. Fundamental change will only come through techniques of invasion and insurgency. These concepts need to be related to his idea of learning systems. This will now be attempted by developing the idea of a functional adult education system.

A FUNCTIONAL ADULT EDUCATION SYSTEM

In attempting to provide a conceptual basis on which to construct an adult education system for the 1980s and beyond it is necessary to turn initially to the experiments in adult education provision which were reported earlier.

In summarising his Liverpool experience Lovett has pointed to the 'fragmented, disjointed nature of existing adult education provision' and recommends that if it was intended to repeat the exercise generally there would be a need for 'much more co-ordination between all of the bodies involved in adult education than is at present the case'.[6] Such co-ordination would of course be necessary at an organisational level and, more importantly, at field level; 'Formal institutional committee structures involving all the bodies concerned with adult education are no substitute for informal network systems, where a number of field workers act as network agents on the ground, concentrating on the *central nature of the educational service* rather than any particular form' [my emphasis].[7]

Fordham *et al* similarly argue for co-ordination through frequent meetings between representatives of agencies which 'encourage professionals involved in the health, education and social service departments to view each other's services as resources to be developed and utilised in an inter-disciplinary way'.[8] They suggest the setting up of neighbourhood adult education resource centres as a base for an outreach worker and his support group. Presumably as we are told that much of the new work will have to be developed in the LEA sector, such centres would usually be local authority funded and staffed.

The arguments for inter-agency co-ordination and concentration on the *'central nature of the education service'* need to be taken to their logical conclusion, that is to the concept of a *functional adult education system*. Such a system needs to be able to respond to the educational needs of all adults whether they are concerned, for example, with an issue adversely affecting their quality of life, or with a wish to learn to cook or play badminton, or with access to higher education or retraining. Such a comprehensive service requires a combining of the talents and resources of all providers well beyond co-ordination or lunchtime meetings – we are all currently operating within different areas of what should be a single functional adult education system. Working in isolation existing institutions are inadequate to the tasks which face the education service: in Schon's terms there is 'a state of mismatch between the institutional map and the array of problems taken to be important'; furthermore, 'in the realm of social design we see that we cannot resolve mismatches at any level short of broad functional systems'.[9]

Existing practice is not favourable to such a development. Nevertheless if adult educators are sincere in their commitment to broaden access to the service they must subject both their practice and their attitudes to critical scrutiny. The present picture, with few exceptions, is of the different providers doing their 'thing' in isolation. What each does is similar yet different, reflecting their different histories and the resources at their disposal. There is some co-operative effort; universities and the WEA mount joint courses; LEAs and universities co-operate in training schemes for teachers of adults. All kinds of practitioners meet on conferences and express joint concern about the narrow recruitment base of their work – they must now stop talking and act in a concerted way. What is required are *joint teams of providers at the field work level*, learning together about their communities and about each other and applying the resources of their various institutions to the educational needs identified.

These teams of detached field workers should represent all the current major providers, the LEAs, the WEA, the universities and the polytechnics. Teams need not have the same composition and in any particular area arrangements would reflect local needs and experience. But there must be at least two field workers from different providers, preferably three or four. Such appointments would have to reflect all the lessons to be learned from recent and current experiments in organisational outreach in adult education, that is, the complex role demands made on incumbents, the need for a strong support group and resource centre and for supportive administrative arrangements. The following expansion of the idea of joint fieldwork teams incorporates all these features.

The mutual support existing in such a team would need to be reinforced by a support group involving the caring services, local politicians, schools, industry and voluntary organisations including the trade unions. Whatever message is brought to the fieldwork team or its support group will then find a response. Practitioners operating within a functional service will require a task force mentality, learning as they go but learning jointly. The question, is it adult education? will no longer be very relevant. If an identified adult need calls for an educational response then it is a case of deciding who could best provide. If the appropriate response lies outside the educational service then the message will not be ignored but an answer sought in the support group or within its associated networks; if one is not forthcoming then something has been learned and the group or its networks will have to be strengthened.

In this way existing perceptions of organisational boundaries will be challenged and eventually modified. Slowly the defence of 'jealously guarded territories' will be broken down. Some boundaries will disappear within the framework of an emerging functional education service. By involving school teachers in the support process it will be possible to begin the necessary process of educating them to the need for changes in their own system; they may come to understand that 'early experiences of education largely determine whether later opportunities are taken up or not'.[10] It should certainly be possible to move towards the removing of the attitudinal barriers which impede the effective dual use of school premises.

It is not only current practice but also current attitudes which are not propitious for such an undertaking. University staff sometimes talk and act in a way which suggests that theirs is a somewhat superior 'academic' service and that the WEA provides something of a lower academic status and the LEAs cater merely for recreational and social needs. For their part local authority and WEA staff sometimes, with justification, resent the attitudes of university adult educators. Polytechnics and universities are often not even talking to one another. That the various services are different in some ways is beyond doubt, but essentially in a functional system they would complement each other: *their complementarity needs to find formal expression in joint learning and action at the field level. As a result of working together, complementarity will become interdependence – they will be laying the foundations for a functional adult education system.* Such a partnership would have several consequences:

1. There would be a mutually supportive team of adult educators.
2. Problems and disappointments could be shared and tackled by the joint talents of the team.
3. Continuity would be assured in the event of one of the team leaving.
4. Existing resources could be used more effectively. Extramural and LEA centre accommodation, for example, stands idle for not inconsiderable periods of time and could be more intensively used by a developing service. A practitioner will spend much time building up a social network appropriate to a particular part of his provision – others could short-circuit this process by being introduced into an established network. Thus LEA and extramural staff have independently cultivated the same kinds of network in developing pre-retirement and shop stewards' courses respectively. The industrial and trade union networks of the WEA have been invaluable to university departments. Increasingly there is overlap in the networks necessary to support LEA work, for example, with

'deprived' mothers, single parent families, the unemployed and prisoners, and university and polytechnic programmes with social workers and prison and probation officers.

5. Not only could existing resources be used more effectively but there is a strong probability that a partnership would be better placed to gain access to other than strictly educational funds than if each provider goes it alone.

6. The diversity of the present service, which ought to be its strength, is a major weakness in that it has produced separateness. Political muscle will come from a combining of forces.

7. The learning taking place at field level, fed into resource agencies such as colleges, schools, polytechnics and universities, would provide the reasons and impetus for change in these institutions. Change would probably be slow in coming but a steady process of attrition will effect change. Such change would be facilitated by the presence of adult educators trained in the skills of change management.

Where should such a learning group be located? The inadvisability of locating within a host institution has been demonstrated; adult education is just not 'big' enough to compete within host systems for resources. A lengthy learning period is needed in which the service grows on its own *adult* terms unemcumbered by the needs of children or adolescents. *Ideal concepts of a comprehensive education service encompassing all age groups, though desirable in the long term, ignore the political framework within which the adult education service has to function – it ignores the greater power and social approval of those services with which it is linked.* Given the typical autonomy of school heads and college principals too much depends on their individual attitudes to adult education; usually they are blinkered in their outlook conditioned by society's educational priorities, by their training and by the sheer weight of opinion of the non-adult educators working in the institution. Neither edicts from senior officers in the local authority nor good intentions can solve the problems at the institutional level.

It is on this point that the ideas of those who identify a comprehensive service based on the community school break down. Thus Flude and Parrott, who would site their 'local centres which will be both providers of courses and access points to the system as a whole'[10] within community schools, are condemning their admirable ideas to failure (except possibly in schools in which they or some like-minded proponents hold senior positions). Though they acknowledge that 'as a concept [community education] is imprecise, and as an activity it seems frequently to have promised more than in fact it has delivered', they still hope that 'joint management' schemes can solve operating problems. Success would depend on their being 'no advance assumptions about priorities'.[11] This is politically naïve. They further acknowledge that attitudes will have to change at all levels in the school – attitude change is a notoriously difficult exercise. The vision has to be separated from the reality.

A further criticism of such schemes is that their benefits will accrue primarily to current and future generations of schoolchildren. But what of the several generations of adults whose needs exist now? Change is needed today and the first priority is *a comprehensive service for adults which might then become an equal partner in the development of a lifelong learning system.* Therefore I am arguing for an independent, frontline, 'specialised' adult education service which uses colleges, schools, universities, polytechnics, the WEA and other agencies, as resources. Such a service would be manned by workers drawn from existing providers who would volunteer for the demanding role of frontline worker or network agent. They would need a work base with some accommodation of their own but not in a school or college; such a base would become a resource centre for the local community, a 'neighbourhood adult centre' as envisaged in the Southampton report, or Flude and Parrott's 'educational service station'. The centre would require adequate administrative and caretaking staff who would ensure that the adult educators were left free to use their time in developmental and educational activity.

The Liverpool and Southampton studies both suggest that such an exercise would be expensive; Fordham *et al* see particular difficulties given present funding arrangements. Where are the funds for such an enterprise to be found? Initially there is need for LEAs, the WEA, university departments and polytechnics to release existing staff for the learning role, senior staff with many years' adult education experience who know the service well and have standing within it at local level. A university department should experience no difficulty in releasing a member of staff for what, in effect, would be an action research programme. WEA districts, with less generous staffing levels, might have problems though they did make Tom Lovett available for the Liverpool project – a precedent already exists. Many LEAs should be able to release an experienced adult educator, given that many are currently underemployed.

Central government funds would be needed to prime the exercise on the model of the national literacy campaign but this would not be costly in the context of a total national education budget. Accountability could be achieved by the active involvement of HMIs, as in the Liverpool programme and in the Mee and Wiltshire research. This is not to suggest that the Department of Education and Science is likely to be the only source of funding – among others the Departments of Employment and Health and Social Security should also be involved. A functional system, at a local level, will inevitably involve many presently separated areas of government in jointly co-ordinated research and action. Organisational boundaries will be crossed at all levels in the political superstructure.

Initially a limited number, possibly ten or twelve, teams should be set up as action research groups. The location of these should be determined on the basis of a desire to learn from local studies, in order to build up a fund of transferable knowledge and experience which could guide action in comparable areas in the United Kingdom. Among the criteria for selection of areas would be population density, level of unemployment, degree of owner-occupation, degree of urbanisation and the presence of ethnic minorities. Local authorities in conjunction with universities, polytechnics and the WEA should be asked to tender for central government funding on the basis of jointly designed schemes. These schemes should not be drawn up by local authority officers or institutional directorates but by adult education practitioners. Having to make out a joint case would be an important determinant of where funds were eventually allocated – an effective scheme would indicate a willingness and ability to work together, a critical requirement if the joint teams are to function successfully.

The learning process already begun by the designing of schemes should be furthered by bringing together all of the local teams for joint training. It is likely that the relevant training skills would be present in the group itself, though the combined resources of all the agencies and organisations involved could be drawn on. This would probably have to be a two-stage process with an initial determination of content and source of training skills, followed by a longer period concerned with developing those skills. One advantage of a local team is that any skills deficiency in one member can probably be compensated for by those of another.

Lovett has suggested an outline syllabus for the complexity of roles demanded;

> . . . training would attempt to bring together the best in primary school methods, community development skills, group work practices, creative use of the mass media, knowledge of working class and popular culture, as well as some of the radical ideas and practices of the deschoolers and Third World educationalists like Illich and Freire.[12]

His observations have to be seen within the context of the Educational Priority Area project and his own ideology. Nevertheless many of his recommendations have a more general relevance and both the Liverpool and Southampton reports would be essential reading. Another important area of study would be organisation structures and the process of change within them; Donald Schon would be essential reading here. Interpersonal skills and change management skills training would also be included. Other needs would be revealed by experience and would be responded to on a local or national basis. Once functioning the local teams would not work in isolation; a condition of the funding would be that they came together at frequent intervals in order to learn from each other.

Learning would lead to action. Much of such action could not be expected to meet the standard administrative criteria. However some responses would not necessarily be threatened by such criteria; facilitating access to retraining, to qualifications or to higher education might simply mean bringing individuals into contact with existing opportunities. Some groups in need of role education will be in a position to pay for the services they require; indeed some might pay an economic price which could subsidise other activities. The freedom to charge a fee or not, to have discretion in the use of funds, requires the maximum autonomy possible for the fieldwork team. They would be accountable to the support group for their actions who would have the difficult problem of striking an appropriate balance between support and interference. Their essential function would be to protect the fieldwork team from pressures which would inhibit the work, to play the kind of political role which for example, teachers' unions do in defence of the school system. At the present time the adult service does not have an effective political voice either at local or national level – the individual champion for the cause, such as a college principal, is no substitute for an effective lobby.

The support group will not be a committee-like structure with a constitution and established representation. Some agencies select themselves for membership and those have already been identified. But the support group is also engaged in a learning process and must therefore have the power to co-opt and to invite individuals and groups to join them; it will be continually engaged in redrawing its own boundary. That sub-groups will appear to support certain developments is beyond doubt but it is impossible to forecast what these will be; that such sub-groups should also disband as they achieve their objective is also desirable and should be an expectation within the group when it is formed.

The learning taking place in the field will, where appropriate, be fed into existing organisations such as schools, colleges, the WEA, voluntary organisations, universities and polytechnics, which will have to change in order to accommodate much of the learning. Some messages may call for changes, for example, in attitudes or goals or both. It has already been suggested that such changes are difficult to bring about and will not only take time but will also call for techniques of 'invasion and insurgency'. In developing these concepts Schon identifies several roles which are likely to be very relevant to the approach of the field-work team:

- The guerrilla, the champion gone underground, who tries to subvert the existing institution through informal channels.
- The advocate, who represents and seeks a voice for the powerless
- The organiser, who unites individuals around issues of common concern in order to bring pressures to bear on established institutions.[13]

The adult educator who volunteers for the field role has in effect 'gone underground' in the sense that he is no longer visible or is as visible as he chooses to be. He is in a frontline situation taking his own initiatives of which others, outside the immediate fieldwork group, have little or no knowledge. But he still retains his 'informal' contacts within the 'established institution', he knows where support might lie and how best to influence thinking and decision-making. The 'advocate' and 'organiser' roles clearly overlap; even the powerless find strength if they become organised and their weakness is strongly and publicly expressed as a group characteristic.

The role of the support group in the area of invasion and insurgency will be crucial. As a group they will undergo a unique collective learning experience, they will learn about problems and needs in their community and about the ability of others to respond; they will also learn how others perceive the service they represent, about it strengths and shortcomings. The re-thinking which occurs will have the collective approval of the group and will reinforce their attempts to re-educate their own organisations. Where the composition of participatory committees or councils of educational organisations have been changed in the way suggested in the previous chapter this will greatly assist the process. The same agencies will be represented in both the support group and in the committees and it is likely in some instances that the same persons will serve in both capacities. Thus the argument for change within such committees will be expressed by several members.

In this way what may be an important arena for decision making in institutions will have been 'invaded' – the guerrillas will be inside the organisation in some strength acting as agents for change. This process can be further reinforced if the support group seeks the direct involvement in its work of organisational employees; as many as possible need to be co-opted into task-group activities in the field. In this way the support group can become a training camp for insurgents whose commitment to change will be reinforced by their involvement in identifying the need for it; they will carry this commitment back into their organisational roles. Thus pressures for change will exist at both committee and employee level.

How might this process of influencing change occur in an LEA institution? A college of further education is a useful example, though a comparable process may also occur in other organisational settings. In a college the decision-making hierarchy will consist of a principal, vice-principal and heads of departments, who will meet regularly, usually once a week. The principal will be advised by an academic board consisting of members of staff. Where the balance of power will lie in such a system will vary from institution to institution but its location is likely to be known and understood by an experienced and senior member of staff seconded to the fieldwork team. Straddling the boundary between the college and its community will be a number of advisory committees, reflecting departmental specialisms, whose task it is to advise the Board of Governors. The latter, appointed by the LEA, represent a fairly broad range of community interests.

Within such a complex decision-making system there will be many opportunities for the fieldworker to operate as an 'insurgent'; exerting influence in appropriate areas; knowing where he can appeal for support among staff, students, advisory board members and governors. Other members of staff will be temporarily co-opted by the support group and it is also likely that some advisers or governors will be members of that group. Where there are other adult educators working within the organisation they can operate as a significant pressure group.

Change in one institution will help to create an environment for change in others: emulation is a powerful motive. In colleges of further education for example, work with new groups of students has been quickly taken up by others and not only within the same authority; for example, with the elderly, the physically and mentally handicapped and disadvantaged mothers.

It is arguable that opposition to change may come from the LEA itself. However, this is unlikely given their initial commitment to the outreach programme, the autonomy of college principals supported by their governors, and the development of a strong political lobby within the support group.

The same kind of process could occur within a university or a polytechnic, though the latter does have, in common with colleges of further education, a major advantage over the former: it is service-oriented and has developed by identifying and responding to opportunities present in the community. In contrast a university tends to be isolated from its immediate community and region, though this is truer of the academic and administrative staff than the undergraduate student body. An extramural department which could operate as an effective link between a community and the university rarely does so. It goes out from the university, often in detached centres, but armed only with a single technology of the weekly tutorial group or possibly some simple variation on this requiring, for example, residence. There may be rare exceptions, but in general extramural departments are inadequate to the task of either taking the university and its resources out into its region or bringing community needs back inside the university.

Change is therefore likely to come more slowly in universities than in the polytechnics and colleges of further education, except possibly where there is a substantial fall in undergraduate intake. If jobs are threatened there will be an impetus for change, for serving new publics. Even then, however, it may be necessary for more extramural staff to be located on campus rather than out 'in the sticks'; they may have to 'invade' the university in as great a strength as possible. If they are not inside the institution it is difficult to see how they can influence change. Extramural staff have tended to become separated from their parent institution and 'insurgency' requires a positive and active presence within the organisation. If a university adult educator is detached to work in the field team his ability to influence the whole organisation of which he is ostensibly a part is likely to be much less than that of an LEA colleague. Possibly the most effective strategy would be to involve as many intramural staff as possible in the work of the support group.

No attempt will be made here to summarise the arguments presented in this chapter. In some ways it represents both a summary and a conclusion of much that has gone before. However in order to assist the reader the next chapter, 'Conclusion', presents a summary in diagram form of the model for a functional adult education system.

REFERENCES

1. Toffler, A. (1970) *Future Shock*, Bodley Head: London, p. 129.
2. Schon, Donald A. (1971) *Beyond the Stable State*, M. Temple-Smith: London; Penguin: Harmondsworth, p. 49.
3. *Ibid*. p. 47.
4. *Ibid*. p. 56.
5. Occasionally non-specialised providers such as colleges of further education or community schools provide evidence of substantial innovation outside of traditional organisational boundaries. One such example is the Hinckley College of Further Education (Leicestershire) where a limited traditional programme has been developed in a few years into a broadly based, imaginative, community provision. This example lends support to the view of the importance of a particular individual, in this case a principal with a broad vision of a college as a community resource.
6. Lovett, Tom (1975) *Adult Education, Community Development and the Working Class*, Ward Lock: London, p. 41.
7. *Ibid*. p. 148.
8. Fordham, P., Poulton, G. and Randle, R. (1979) *Learning Networks in Adult Education*, Routledge: London, p. 231.
9. Schon, p. 170.
10. Flude, R. and Parrott, A. (1979) *Education and the Challenge of Change*, Open University Press: Milton Keynes, p. 63.
11. *Ibid*. pp. 132, 134.
12. Lovett, p. 146.
13. Schon, p. 55.

CHAPTER NINE

Conclusion: a model for the development of a functional adult education system

It is appropriate that the experience of the Inner London Education Authority's outreach workers should provide a focus for this conclusion. A decade's experience

has made it possible for the Authority and its outreach workers to realise the magnitude of the task of transforming an educational system into one which is responsive to the whole community. We have come to see that such a task cannot be accomplished by junior staff isolated within a small sector of the education system. Rather, the way forward must lie in a co-ordinated attempt by members, administrators, the inspectorate and staff at all levels and in all branches of the education service to transform that service.

Transforming an educational system can only succeed if all those involved co-ordinate their efforts; it cannot be achieved by junior staff working in isolation. Such testimony, based on extensive experience, has strongly influenced much of the argument presented in this book.

Certain other ideas have been implicit and these may be summarised as follows.

1. There is a need for a *comprehensive education service for adults*, whatever the demands they would make on such a service.
2. *No single type of organisation can be all things to all men*: there are no institutional panaceas. There are many kinds of institution claiming expertise in some aspects of the education of adults: all have something to offer but the contribution of each can be maximised only if they are related to each other within a functional adult education service.
3. *There are many educational needs of adults which are as yet unknown*. Others are known about but are not responded to or are ineffectively catered for.

4. *Even if discovered some needs will not be responded to by existing institutions* or inappropriate responses will be tried. *Therefore a new kind of frontline structure is required* which will,

- uncover adults' educational needs
- provide for these needs where no response capacity already exists
- relate needs to existing institutional provision where appropriate
- act as an agent for change within existing institutions.

It has been argued that the time is right for fundamental change. Technological change and the consequent social disruption demand a comprehensive education service for adults. Furthermore the dramatic cuts in the existing LEA service in the 1970s have created both a necessity and a climate for government initiative.

The first essential is to link existing providers into a co-ordinated functional framework. This is no easy task and will not be achieved by setting up, for example, liaison committees; co-operation alone will not provide either the impetus or the energy for change. The answer lies in joint effort at fieldwork level. Existing practitioners and the organisations from which they are drawn must identify their respective roles within an emerging framework of adult needs which they jointly discover. Teams of senior practitioners need to be detached from their parent institutions to work in frontline situations behind a protective screen provided by a support group consisting not only of representatives of those institutions but also elected members of local authorities and representatives of voluntary organisations, industry, trade unions and the health, social and probationary services. Not only will the support group protect the fieldworkers from interference, it will also come to represent a collective political voice for a comprehensive adult education service.

The frontline team needs a resource base under its own control in order to be able to respond to some needs directly. They will relate other needs to existing providers where appropriate. They will not be mere passive channels of communication between individuals or groups and institutions but active 'insurgents', working for change within those institutions – change in priorities, in the allocation of resources and in goals and attitudes. Their efforts will receive strong reinforcement from the support group whose members will also be 'invading' their own organisations and agencies. Further pressure for change will occur because some support group members will be drawn from within existing educational organisations and others will function on advisory or user committees in such institutions.

The resulting functional system is depicted in Figure 4. It represents a

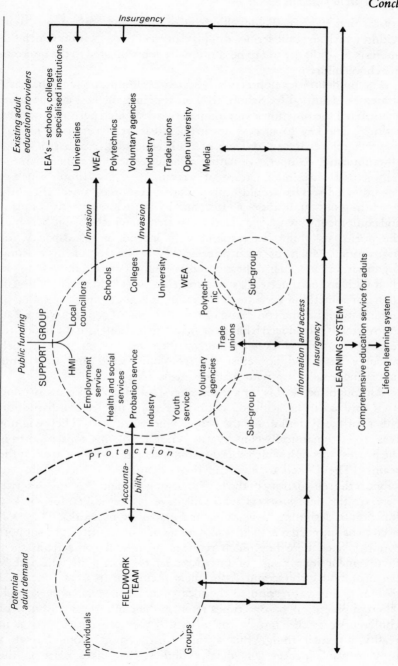

Fig. 4 Model for the development of a functional adult education system: structure and process

critical first stage in the development of a lifelong education system within which an adult service can play an *equal* part – within which the interests of adults are not to be continually subordinated to the interests of schoolchildren.

The model of development advocated exemplifies one of the basic strategies identified by Schon, to 'knit together the still autonomous elements of the functional system in networks which permit concerted action'.[1] The key to success lies in the creation of networks linking together the separate providers of adult education, emphasising 'the all-embracing, co-operative nature of adult education rather than the fragmented, disjointed nature of existing . . . provision';[2] such a co-ordinated service would utilise existing resources more efficiently by cutting out duplication of effort and by more intensive use of plant and equipment. It would be a learning system in which change becomes the norm. Its ability to respond will depend on its capacity for innovation. Much of such capacity is to be found in existing organisations, indeed had these organisations not existed those who pin their faith on social network structures alone would have had to invent them, or something very much like them. It is not simply a question of organisations having command of resources but of continuity; once an innovation is introduced it has to be maintained, built into the structure, leaving frontline workers to pursue their search activities. If such resource bases did not exist the frontline would find their time increasingly taken up with maintenance activity.

Although the need is for a learning system capable of transforming itself this has to be achieved without creating intolerable disruption either for the system or for the people who work in it. 'They will not cease to be dynamically conservative – not if dynamic conservatism is the process through which social systems keep from flying apart at the seams. [They] need to maintain their identity, and their ability to support the self-identity of those who belong to them.'[3] At greatest risk here are the field workers who will have responsibility for the key function of designing, developing and managing networks. They will need to be supported in their search for a sense of security. The support group is vital here but much reinforcement will come from their involvement in a range of interpersonal networks, in which they perform nodal roles, and from their membership of a functional system giving expression to the idea of an *adult education movement*. Though practitioners sometimes refer, in the euphoric atmosphere of conferences, to the 'movement' of which they are a part there is in reality no such thing. But a functional system would create a movement, 'a process of social evolution that takes place in the interstices of established organisations; or rather, established organisations become from time to time the instruments through which the movement works itself out'.[4]

Does the process cease with the establishment of a comprehensive adult system? Schon would suggest not arguing that there will be a tendency for 'functional aggregation'. 'How far up the ladder of aggregation is it possible to go?',[5] he asks. The answer for adult education is that once it has become politically established, when it has achieved the social approval and status of other sectors of education, it can become an *equal* partner in a functional education system for all ages whatever its label, lifelong, continuing . . .[6]

REFERENCES

1. Schon, Donald A. (1971) *Beyond the Stable State*, M. Temple-Smith: London; Penguin: Harmondsworth, p. 171.
2. Lovett, Tom (1975) *Adult Education, Community Development and the Working Class*, Ward Lock: London, p. 46.
3. Schon, p. 57.
4. *Ibid.*, p. 104.
5. *Ibid.*, pp. 172–3.
6. Those readers who wish to develop further their understanding of how organisations learn are recommended to read, Argyris, C. and Schon, D. A. (1978) *Organisational Learning: a Theory of Action Perspective*, Addison-Wesley: Reading (Massachusetts).

CHAPTER TEN

Postscript: a profession of adult education?

The reader may have been surprised that in a book utilising a framework of concepts drawn from the sociology of organisations there has been only passing reference to the idea of a profession. Indeed, for many years, I have used the idea with adult educators who have found it useful in conceptualising and organising their attitudes and experience. The interest of practitioners is understandable. Their work is frequently regarded as being marginal by other educators and by their employers; not unnaturally they look at the status enjoyed by those groups able to substantiate their claim to professional standing in society.

Increasingly, however, doubts have intruded about its relevance to an understanding of the tasks to be faced by an adult education service in the 1980s and beyond. A professionally dominated service has seemed more and more irrelevant. Nevertheless it is possible and appropriate to utilise a somewhat brief analysis of the concept in order to identify the cause of the doubts. Therefore, there is no intention to review the quite extensive literature on the sociology of the professions but merely to utilise some aspects which have been found to be particularly useful to adult educators. We are not concerned with the question (which undoubtedly still interests some practitioners however) is adult education a profession? The essential question is how might the study of professions and of professionals improve our understanding of the role of the adult educator?

It was suggested in chapter 4 that the practitioner is making a professional judgement when he decides to ignore or manipulate administrative regulations; the concept was used to describe an act which was in the interests of students; for example, allowing a class to continue to meet even though it fell short of minimum attendance requirements. This service-to-client ethic is said to be but one characteristic of occupational groups usually described as professions such as law and medicine. Many writers have seen the search for such essential characteristics as the appropriate methodology in attempting to define the concept. Though the resulting 'trait' models of professions have been subject to much criticism[1] they have, nevertheless, been found to be a useful starting point for adult educators.

A basic weakness of the traits approach is said to be that few seem to be able to agree on what the core characteristics are. Thus Millerson researched the literature and came to the conclusion that, 'Of the dozens of writers on this subject few seem to be able to agree on the real determinants of professional status'.[2] He identified twenty-three different 'elements' which various authors have included in their definitions.[3] Despite the fact that no two of the writers are totally in agreement on the combination of elements which constitute a profession there are, nevertheless, six characteristics which are much more frequently mentioned than any others:

1. A profession involves a skill based on theoretical knowledge.
2. The skill requires training and education.
3. The professional must demonstrate competence by passing a test.
4. Integrity is maintained by adherence to a code of conduct.
5. The service is for the public good.
6. The profession is organised.

Though adult educators are frequently eager to evaluate their own occupational group against such criteria they are usually disappointed by their conclusions! Nevertheless the exercise invariably stimulates animated discussion and also a search for other conceptual frameworks within which to analyse their role. Johnson has proved useful here with his focus on the power which any occupational group has to control the producer: consumer relationship. He begins with the proposition that; 'In all differentiated societies, the emergence of specialised occupational skills, whether productive of goods or services, creates relationships of *social and economic dependence* and, paradoxically, relationships of *social distance*.'[4]

The stages of his argument can usefully be expressed in diagrammatic form as follows (Fig. 5).

The 'area of uncertainty' is the inevitable consequence of unspecialised consumption. Most of us are conscious of this when faced not only with the diagnosis of a doctor but also that of a motor mechanic when the car breaks down or of the television or washing machine repair man. Most lack the knowledge and skills to challenge

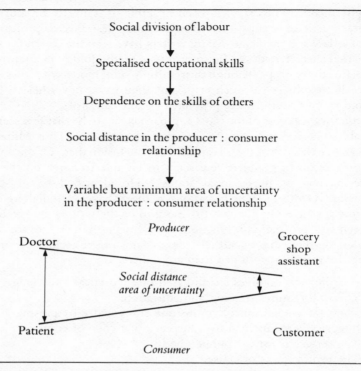

Fig. 5 Social distance in the producer: consumer relationship

the expert in his own field of competence. In such a relationship there exists the possibility of exploitation of the consumer by the producer and the knowledge gap between them creates possibilities for the latter's autonomy. Therefore there is a need for some kind of social control. Johnson suggests that there are three ways in which such control may be effected reflecting a spectrum extending from producer autonomy to consumer control (Fig. 6).

Where does the adult educator belong in this model? Elements of all three types of control appear to be present. There is autonomy in the sense that the practitioner effectively defines needs and how they are to be met by offering a largely unchanging class list – the consumer can choose from this list but his 'needs' are usually responded to by a standard educational package, a class. This standard response reflects the fact that he is also subject to 'mediative' control. His employers approve of the class as the 'unit of production' because it is the generally accepted technology in education: additionally it is more easily controlled within a framework of administrative criteria such as a list of

Producer autonomy		Consumer control
Collegiate control	*Mediative control*	*Patronage*
The producer defines both the needs of the consumer and how they are to be met (e.g. the medical profession).	A third party mediates in the producer : consumer relationship defining both needs and how they are to be met (e.g. a state financed education service employing the producers and supervising the manner in which the service is provided through an inspectorate).	The consumer defines both his own needs and how they are to be met. This may, for example, be an aristocratic patron or corporate patronage (e.g. the accountant employed by an industrial firm). Alternatively it may take the form of *communal control* where consumer organisations set out to try to control the production of goods or services.

Fig. 6 Typology of institutional orders of occupational control[5]

'approved' classes, a list of 'recreational' classes for which a higher fee is charged, minimum attendance requirements, etc. In this way the employer is strongly influencing both what needs are to be met and by what means. There is also an element of 'patronage' in that consumers, by exercising choice, largely determine both the subject content and the balance of a programme of classes.

It is clear that 'social distance' and the 'area of uncertainty' are not the same for all adults. Many for whom education has been a successful experience know the system well and how to manipulate it, know what opportunities exist and how to gain access to them. Their ability to use and influence the system is often enhanced by practitioners who, in keeping with a participative philosophy, deliberately involve students in aspects of decision making. In contrast the 'social distance' between the service and non-users is very great. Very many practitioners wish to see this dramatically reduced, they envisage a service accessible to all adults. But many would acknowledge that such accessibility implies movement away from the professional position of 'collegiate' control to the 'patronage' end of Johnson's typology, that is towards 'communal' control. Diagrammatically this view can be represented as follows: (Fig. 7).

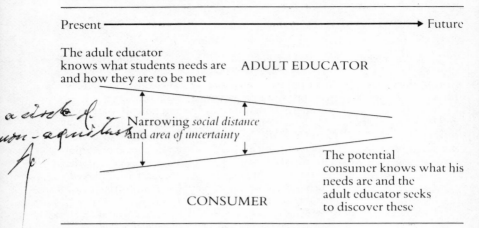

Fig. 7 From professional control to communal control

Such a shift from a practitioner dominated service to one subject to communal control is implicit in the transition from the centre-periphery model of organisations to learning systems. It involves, in Johnson's terms, a move away from professional control, a move which many practitioners are likely to find extremely threatening; (LEA officers and elected members, extra-mural staffs of universities, etc., may also sleep less easily.) It is appropriate here to remind ourselves of the views of Fordham *et al*. They identify 'a matrix of independent learning groups and networks' which offer 'a positive and dynamic alternative to a number of separate professionally dominated and controlled services'. Furthermore a learning approach requires the adult educator 'to eschew control or colonisation' – he must be 'prepared for people to take things into their own hands . . . to direct their own learning'.[6]

If there is to be this move to communal control what role is implied for the adult educator? Fordham *et al* suggest that he must be 'able to relate expertise and knowledge to the social experience and particular needs of people'.[7] It is, therefore, in the application of educational skills and knowledge that his 'professionalism' is still relevant. He has to achieve an understanding of potential learners, their attitudes, knowledge, skills and also of the economic and social environment in which they work and live. Armed with this knowledge of their present state he makes judgements as an educator, who also knows the system and how to use it, and identifies a more desirable situation. He then sets out to help them close the gap.

There are probably those who would not acknowledge and certainly not approve of this educator role – 'desirable' by what and whose criteria?, they might ask. They would identify, for example, the dangers of the practitioner making judgements from within a middle-class framework of reference on behalf of working class participants. The logic of the learning approach is, however, that 'desirability', should be a matter for joint determination. If there is agreement about a more desirable state of affairs it is certain that the adult educator can markedly facilitate the process of getting there given, for example, his knowledge of the agencies which might contribute and of learning methodology.

It is probably inevitable that those who experience feelings of marginality, who find that their work is little esteemed by others, should sometimes cast envious glances in the direction of occupational groups having established social status and a large measure of autonomy. It is suggested here, however, that they are looking in the wrong direction. Professionally controlled services are inimical to the development of a comprehensive service relevant and accessible to all adults; practitioners will need to identify not with the collegiate end of the model but with the opposed position of communal control.

REFERENCES

1. See Johnson, T. J. (1972) *Professions and Power*, Macmillan: London, Chs 1 and 2, for an effective critique of the 'traits' approach.
2. Millerson, G. (1964) 'Dilemmas of professionalism', *New Society* **4** (June), p. 15.
3. Millerson, G. (1964) *The Qualifying Associations*, Routledge: London, p. 5.
4. Johnson, p. 41.
5. This typology is drawn from Johnson, Ch. 3.
6. Fordham, P., Poulton, G. and Randle, R. (1979) *Learning Networks in Adult Education*, Routledge: London, p. 202.
7. *Ibid*. p. 201.

Bibliography

Ackoff, Russell L. (1974) *Redesigning the Future*, New York.

Argyris, C. (1957) *Personality and Organisation*, New York.

Argyris, C. (1964) *Integrating the Individual and the Organisation*, New York.

Argyris, C. and Schon, D. A. (1978) *Organisational Learning: A Theory of Action Perspective*, Reading (Massachusetts).

Baldridge, J. V. and Deal, T. E. (1975) *Managing Change in Educational Organisations*, Berkeley.

Blau, P. M. and Scott, W. R. (1963) *Formal Organisations*, London.

Burnham, Peter S. (1969) 'Role theory and educational administration', in Baron, G. and Taylor, W. (eds) *Educational Administration and the Social Sciences*, London.

Clark, Burton R. (1956) 'Organisational adaptation and precarious values: a case study', *American Sociological Review*, **21**.

Clark, Burton R. (1958) *The Marginality of Adult Education*, Boston.

Deppe, D. A. (Oct. 1969) 'The adult educator: marginal man and boundary definer', *Adult Leadership*, **18**, No. 4.

Emery, F. and Thorsrud, E. (1976) *Democracy at Work*, Leiden.

Etzioni, A. (1964) *Modern Organisations*, New Jersey.

Flude, R. and Parrott, A. (1979) *Education and the Challenge of Change*, Milton Keynes.

Fordham, P., Poulton, G. and Randle, R. (1979) *Learning Networks in Adult Education*, London.

Freiere, Paulo (1972) *Pedagogy of the Oppressed*, Harmondsworth.

Gross, N., Giacquinta, J. B. and Bernstein, M. (1971) *Implementing Organisational Innovations*, New York.

Herriot, R. E. and Gross, N. (eds) (1979) *The Dynamics of Planned Educational Change*, Berkeley.

Herzberg, F. *et al.* (1959) *The Motivation to Work*, New York.

Hughes, J. T. (1979) *The Provision of Non-Vocational Adult Education by the Nottinghamshire Education Authority 1944 to 1975*, M.Phil. dissertation, University of Nottingham.

Johnson, T. J. (1972) *Professions and Power*, London.

Keddie, N. (1980) 'Adult education: an ideology of individualism' in Thompson, J. L. (ed.) *Adult Education for a Change*, London.

Leigh, J. (1971) *Young People and Leisure*, London.

Lovett, Tom (1975) *Adult Education, Community Development and the Working Class*, London.

Lovett, Tom, and Mackay, L. (1978) 'Community-based study groups – a Northern Ireland case study', *Adult Education*, **51**, No. 1.

Maslow, A. H. (1954) *Motivation and Personality*, New York.

McGregor, D. (1960) *The Human Side of Enterprise*, New York.

Mee, G. and Wiltshire, H. (1978) *Structure and Performance in Adult Education*, London.

Millerson, G. (June 1964) 'Dilemmas of professionalism', *New Society*, **4**.

Millerson, G. (1964) *The Qualifying Associations*, London.

Musgrave, P. W. (Oct. 1973) 'The relationship between school and community: a reconsideration', *Community Development Journal*, **8**, No. 3.

Newman, M. (1979) *The Poor Cousin*, London.

Pollard, Harold R. (1978) *Further Developments in Management Thought*, London.

Russell Report (1973) *Adult Education: A Plan for Development*, HMSO, London.

Schein, Edgar H. (1965) *Organisational Psychology*, New Jersey.

Schon, Donald A. (1971) *Beyond the Stable State*, Harmondsworth.

Selznick, P. (1966) *TVA and the Grass Roots*, New York.

Toffler, A. (1970) *Future Shock*, London.

Watson, G. (1970) 'Resistance to Change', in Bennis, W. G. *et al.* (eds) *The Planning of Change*, London.

Index